Charles A. Tesconi, Jr.
Van Cleve Morris

UNIVERSITY OF ILLINOIS PRESS
Urbana/Chicago/London

THE
Anti-Man Culture

Bureautechnocracy and the Schools

© 1972 by The Board of Trustees of the University of Illinois
Manufactured in the United States of America
Library of Congress Catalog Card No. 75–160385

252 00189 3

TABLE OF CONTENTS

vii

PART TWO / A NEW KIND OF EDUCATION

PREFACE

The distinguishing feature of twentieth-century Western society, particularly the United States, is the imperious influence of the scientific and technological world view—an arrangement of epistemological and normative convictions which specify ways of knowing, the nature of knowledge, and the manner in which knowledge is to be applied to the physical and social world. The pervasive authority of this world view has created a situation wherein science and technology are fast becoming the basic determinants of education and, accordingly, basic determinants of every major social institution. It is our contention that these forces have given rise to a new organizational pattern, a pattern so widespread in our society that it amounts to a new social-cultural milieu. We call this *bureautechnocracy*.

During the last century we have learned how to use science, technology, and organizational principles to persistently improve man's place and prospects in this world. Massive strides in the medical sciences, better health care, increased human support services, relative affluence, wide-ranging choice among consumer goods and services—all these and much more testify to the efficacy of science and technology. And they are responsible for an ever improving physical standard of living. Although we are a long way from eliminating poverty and the attending social-psychological miseries, no one can gainsay the fact that the poor as well as the affluent have benefited from the material wonders of bureautechnocracy.

In spite of all this, a dark cloud of malaise lingers over this society. And this discomfort, expressed through anxiety, alienation, despair, deep intergenerational conflict, and widespread neuroses, follows from the lurking suspicion that the new world of science and technology poses dangerous threats to our personal and collective values and freedoms. We have built and sustained such freedoms through pluralistic forms of private life, diffusion of power among many groups of people, private ownership of decentralized modes of production, protection of the right of privacy, and a guarantee to the individual citizen that he has a right to participate in the institutions and processes of government.

Bureautechnocracy, however, depends and prospers upon contrary tendencies: assimilation and homogenization, concentrated power, corporate ownership, privacy-invading information-gathering agencies, massive and impersonal size, esoteric scientific and technological knowledge, and "expert" decision-making. These latter-day bureautechnocratic imperatives are eating away at the foundations of our freedoms, values, and rights to the realization of human potential.

Upset by such conditions, many scientists and social philosophers are contributing to a growing body of literature which warns of the perils inherent in the rationally organized, science- and technology-dominated society. The more extreme critics unembarrassingly argue that we are rapidly approaching the kind of "dead end" society fictionalized in Orwell's *1984*.

Are the critics, and particularly the doomsday prophets, going too far? Are they caught up in their rhetoric and moral-ideological fervor? Are they projecting upon all of us their own alienation and despair? Perhaps. But their criticisms must be taken seriously, if for no other reason than that their fears are shared by many people in our society.

We must listen. We must begin to understand, to become increasingly aware of the nature and functions of bureautechnocracy and the threats to human dignity and freedom which it generates. We must begin to understand how bureautechnocracy creates and sustains pressures which lead to alienation and lost self-esteem. We must begin to understand the ways in which bureautechnocracy creates and comes to depend upon a class of experts who profoundly influence the nature, direction, and values of our society. We must begin to understand how bureautechnocracy tramples upon the grounds of human feeling and personal knowledge. And we must begin to exercise our freedom in seeking ways to protect ourselves from the dangerous consequences of bureautechnocracy and to overcome those elements therein which have occasioned the frightening conditions themselves. This book is an attempt to deal with these imperatives.

In the analysis of these imperatives, it is important to remember that no examination of American social conditions deserves listening to unless it issues in suggested lines of corrective social action. Since education in the United States has been advertised for so long as the reflecting mirror of what we consider best in our society, it is little wonder that these social therapies often turn to the American school as the place where some new directions can be plotted. In our development of the argument, we have tried to be faithful to this strategic requirement of the social commentator. But in our case, the school represents an ambiguous starting-place for reform, for in the following pages we are not merely saying that American social life has run into trouble from which it may be rescued by the school. Rather, we are saying that the school itself is part of the trouble, and that it must be rescued from itself!

Why is it, for example, that first-graders generally enjoy going to school but twelfth-graders do not? We believe it can be traced to the increasing bureaucratization of educational institutions in direct correlation with the age of the student clientele. Why do so many youngsters in our schools and colleges fail to achieve anywhere near their maximum capacities? We believe it has something to do with the ruthless depersonalization of today's teaching, in which teachers deal with their students as so much office help. Why do affluent, middle-class college students raise such hell on our campuses? We believe it is directly connected to the college professor's stubborn belief that knowledge is always some pure, objective, scientific body of fact which bears some metaphysical relationship to the "real world" that exists beyond the reach of human feeling and which can be organized into corporate departments of instruction like a business downtown.

The school, from kindergarten to graduate school, is part of the problem. Indeed, it may be the center of the problem. And it is altogether possible that reform, like charity, should begin at home.

In accord with this angle of approach, *The Anti-Man Culture* is divided into two parts. Part I is given over to an analysis of the nature and origins of bureautechnocracy, its conspicuous consequences, its major social imperatives, its frightening impact on human dignity, its supporting ideology, the widespread extension of its basic support—the scientific world view.

Part II is addressed to the bureautechnocratization of the school and a description and analysis of what amounts to a new epistemology—a new way of looking at knowing and knowledge —and how this new epistemology can be put into operation in our schools and colleges.

This book, then, is an attempt at both diagnosis and prescription. The former reveals major social and intellectual developments of our time, their insidious consequences, and the supporting role of education. The latter offers a way out of the educational morass, a way of making the schools a place where children and youth learn to deal honestly with themselves and others, and with the depersonalizing demands of a bureautechnocratic society. Perhaps such learning can eventually serve to make this a better place in which to live.

CHARLES A. TESCONI, JR.
VAN CLEVE MORRIS

Chicago
January, 1971

ACKNOWLEDGMENTS

The ideas that have found their way into these pages have come from a number of different sources—the books we have read, the people we have talked to, and the sheer experience of living through these times. As for the documentable sources, we have acknowledged them throughout the book. During the writing, colleagues Frederick David Erickson, Donald R. Warren, and Kenneth R. Johnson all provided criticisms and suggestions which served to make this a tighter and more persuasive argument.

We wish also to credit our students who have listened courteously, but without intimidation, as these ideas have been formulated; their reactions and rejoinders have helped to sharpen the line of discussion. Mrs. Flora Costea and Mrs. Sharon Sowa Lindauer, typists with a sure touch and a generosity of overtime energy, prepared the manuscript. Finally, we thank our families, whose patience stretched over several years as this work gradually came into existence.

To all of the above, we say a hearty thank you. For each other, we reserve a quiet, unspoken salute: We have outlasted the vicissitudes of joint authorship, and we stand by the result!

PART ONE
Cultivated Irrationality

CHAPTER 1

Bureautechnocracy: The New Culture

THE MERGER OF BUREAUCRACY AND TECHNOLOGY

Ours is an age in which many of man's most cherished dreams are coming true. The conquest of space, the transmutation of matter, the subjugation of disease, abundant leisure, journeys to the moon and beyond—one by one distant hopes are becoming realities. At the same time, however, widespread poverty, general neuroses, deeply entrenched feelings of dehumanization and alienation, and a prostituted natural environment deaden the satisfaction of dreams fulfilled. And the reality of nuclear weaponry makes a likely eventuality of the prophetic nightmare of an earth wasted by fire.

The irony of these contradictions records itself on the psyche of modern man and is played back to the tune of alienation, anxiety, despair, and mental illness. The evidence is in, and it is explicit: a sociocultural environment produced by man's genius is the breeding ground for defaced human spirits. We call this environment *bureautechnocracy*.

The axial words which constitute the term "bureautechnocracy" refer to a particular genus of social organization (bureau-cracy) on the one hand, and what is customarily referred to as the application of scientific or organized knowledge to practical tasks (technology) on the other. At base, therefore, bureautech-nocracy is that phenomenon of the twentieth century which is the offspring of the marriage of bureaucratic *form* and tech-nological *process*.

Bureaucracy. Bureaucracies are organized social systems wherein tasks are assigned to individuals and to groups so as to attain, efficiently and economically, through the functional co-ordination of all activities, the objectives previously agreed on. Beyond this definitional limit, bureaucracies share the following basic features:

(1) a hierarchized series of offices, each containing an area of imputed competence, responsibility, and status, ra-tionally organized and functionally related for the pur-pose of achieving maximum efficiency in attaining pre-determined goals;

(2) an impersonal, routinized structure defined by syste-matic rules wherein legitimized authority rests in the roles or offices thereof and not in the person of the role/office incumbent;

(3) prescribed relations between various offices involving a considerable degree of formality and clearly defined so-cial distance between occupants of these offices;

(4) systematic rules aimed at minimizing friction and official contact between office incumbents to patterns which pro-duce a stable set of mutual expectations.

Consider the U.S. Army. This social system with its standard-ized tables of organization, prescribed goals, elaborate and formalized arrangement of personnel, equipment, machinery, and processes, and its prescribed hierarchy of ranked roles and offices, epitomizes bureaucratic social systems. The relationships between persons of different rank are clearly spelled out by the rules of the military. Commissioned officers, noncommissioned officers, and those of lower rank have responsibilities which are clearly defined and functionally related to one another. Procedures for dealing with any task, problem, etc., are predetermined by the rules of the organization. In any case, bureaucracies share characteristics suggested by these words and phrases: rational, functional, organized, specialized, prescribed goals, systematic, efficient, impersonal, routinized, hierachized statuses, specific rules, prescribed relationships, formality, social distance, complicated social ritual, pecking order, minimized friction, stability, and mutual expectations.

It takes no great insight to recognize that, as a form of social organization, bureaucracy is a prevailing trend in modern society. Whether we are talking about school, government, church, industry, baseball, unions, or the military, it is almost impossible not to be talking about bureaucracy. All of us have contact with bureaucracy. And whether such contact is through our roles as workers, students, consumers, or all these combined, a fact of contemporary life is that such contact is increasingly extensive and intensive.

Technology. The other pivotal rootword of bureautechnocracy is commonly defined as the systematic application of scientific or other organized knowledge to practical tasks. There are, of course, numerous technologies. Each, however, is a function of the type of knowledge being applied and, more important, the nature of that to which the knowledge is applied. Thus, "Dental Technology" is the systematic or methodical application of organized knowledge (derived from many fields of knowledge ranging from tool-and-dye engineering to medical science) to the practical tasks associated with "doing" dentistry. Computer technology is the systematic application of knowledge, from many fields, to the practical tasks associated with the workings and effects of computers.

Our concern is not with different individual technologies.

There are too many to come to know individually. We are interested, rather, in that which is common to the numerous technologies, to which they all owe their essential qualities, and that which we take as the most appropriate definition of technology: *the deliberate, rationalized, and standardized application of organized knowledge for the purpose of attaining some predetermined end.*[1] Technology (through technologists) does not leave matters to feeling, inspiration, intuition, or even ingenuity in applying knowledge to some practical task. Instead, technology transforms nonreflective behavior into behavior that is methodical and formalized. It standardizes our world and ritualizes our responses to that world.

It is a commonplace that technology is entering, has entered, into virtually every area of life. An advanced industrialized society is committed to the quest for *continually improved means* to predetermined ends and, accordingly, for a civilization increasingly accustomed to standardization and regulation. Government is continually searching for ways by which records can be more efficiently and economically compiled and stored. Educational institutions are perpetually seeking procedures which would eliminate the myriad problems associated with handling entrance applications, reviewing applicants, and enrolling students in courses. Corporations are perennially looking for ways to reduce expenditures and increase profits. In short, contemporary society is increasingly concerned with the elimination of irrational, nonrational, inspirational, ingenious, intuitive, nonstandardized approaches to human activity. Technology, as rational and standardized means for achieving preconceived ends, is the vehicle for this quest.

Technology, moreover, is the fuel for its own engine. The introduction of just one technological product, the computer, into the modern bureaucratic model gives rise to a pattern of organization which is dramatically different from the original. Instead

[1] Our definition is very close to what Jacques Ellul, in *The Technological Society*, calls *technique*.

of merely replacing a human with a computer, management moves toward reorganizing its whole operation, toward rationalizing and technologizing the entire system. Technology is its own imperative; it demands more technology.

With these basic descriptions of bureaucracy and technology, we now see that bureautechnocracy is *a pattern of social management wherein the hierachized, pyramidal, depersonalized model of human organization (bureaucracy) is linked with standardized, rationalized means (technology) with the overall aim of achieving control, flexibility, and efficiency in reaching some commercial or social objective.* The bureaucratic model described earlier, as a "pure" organizational form, is out of joint with the complex demands of advanced industrialized society. Rapid and extensive change, increased interdependency among social institutions and processes, and the vigor with which scientific technology has crept into every corner of human activity have created a social environment so complex that the bureaucratic form, as such, is no longer sustaining itself. Bureaucracy can no longer be viewed as something separate from technology, and the complexity of the latter is such that it can only flourish when merged with bureaucratic structure. The result is a new organizational form.

The marriage of structure and process, this bringing together of two powerful social inventions into a single instrument, has captured the American imagination as the single best method of dealing with virtually every problem that confronts us as a people. As the imperium of methodologies, it is now shaping its master into its own image. It is converting human beings into bureautechnocratic instruments.

By way of illustration, bureautechnocratic systems are now so pervasive that taken together they combine to produce an environment. As an environment, a kind of psychic ecology, bureautechnocracy is so arranged that man can increasingly confront his physical and social world without scraping against cutting surfaces. Bureautechnocracy arranges, organizes, rationalizes, and standardizes in such an all-encompassing way that little is left to chance or human subjectivity. It smooths the pathways of decision-making with a view to reducing shock, conflict, and reflective adjustment. And in the process, as we shall see, bureautechnocracy protects itself and insures its continued growth.

The corporation epitomizes bureautechnocracy and illustrates how the system of bureautechnocracy has evolved into environment. A corporation is a legal entity chartered or authorized by a state or federal government to engage in specified activities. A business corporation, in particular, is a manufacturing, commercial, or financial firm given legally authorized existence, thereby allowing a group of individuals to conduct business. Each corporation is not only an organization performing some specialized function in the complicated workings of an industrial society, but it is also organized on the basis of a system of graded positions which carry differential responsibilities, rewards, and prestige. The internal arrangements of the corporation, its system of reward and prestige, and its ability to focus its energies on long-range objectives serve to highlight its "system character." Furthermore, the corporation's success in meshing form and process is indicative of its bureautechnocratic character.

Corporate expansion and the concentration of numerous markets under one roof typify bureautechnocracy as environment. Our economic structure is dominated by a very few giant corporations, all eminently bureautechnocratic in nature. For example, *Fortune* magazine's annual listing of the top 500 industrial firms in 1968[2] showed that these firms accounted for close to 64 percent of all industrial sales in the United States. In their fields, the top 500 employed 687 out of every 1,000 workers in 1968.[3] In our country, 95 percent of the business firms have fewer than twenty employees, but such firms account for fewer than one-fourth of the wage earners and salaried workers in the economy;

[2] Top ten: General Motors, Standard Oil of New Jersey, Ford, General Electric, Chrysler, IBM, Mobil Oil, Texaco, Gulf Oil, and U.S. Steel.
[3] *Time*, May, 23, 1969, p. 98.

the other three-fourths are employed by the corporate giants which make up only about 5 percent of the total number of business firms.

> In 1965, three industrial corporations, General Motors, Standard Oil of New Jersey and Ford Motor Company, had more gross income than all of the farms in the country. The income of General Motors, of $20.7 billion, about equalled that of the three million smallest farms in the country, around ninety percent of all farms. The gross revenues of each of the three corporations just mentioned far exceed those of any single state. The revenues of General Motors in 1963 were fifty times those of Nevada, eight times those of New York and slightly less than one-fifth those of the federal government.[4]

The large corporation, through concentration of an ever increasing number of markets under one corporate roof, touches millions upon millions of people, directly or indirectly. The dominating influence of the corporation in our society suggests that, in light of just this one bureautechnocratic social system, opportunities to escape contact with bureautechnocracy are few. Roughly two-thirds of us work for large corporations. All of us buy from them. And all of us are bombarded, through the communicative media if nothing else, with their "progress" reports, sales claims, promotional campaigns, and selling techniques. In short, the role of the corporate structure, as bureautechnocratic system, reflects the prevailing and ubiquitous influence of bureautechnocracy as both system and environment.

The growth and influence of the corporation necessitates, in turn, the creation of a gaggle of governmental agencies. The power which has been placed in these quasi-public corporations has, therefore, given rise to more bureautechnocratic systems at all government levels. This growth has been evidenced in the initial response of governmental agencies to corporate growth

[4] John Kenneth Galbraith, *The New Industrial State* (New York: New American Library, 1967), p. 87.

and power; this response has been, largely, in the area of control. We now see, for example, governmental efforts to regulate "the total income available for the purchase of goods and services in the economy. It seeks to insure sufficient purchasing power to buy whatever the current labor force can produce. And, more tentatively and with considerably less sanction in public attitudes, it seeks, given the resulting high employment, to keep wages from shoving up prices and prices from forcing up wages in a persistent upward spiral."[5]

Governmental response to corporate influence is not always aimed at circumscribing corporate functions or controlling marketplace activities. Government also responds by way of cooperation and integration of aims and activities. This usually takes place between government and the largest corporations, the result being an increasing overall integration of bureautechnocratic systems. Recently expressed fears about the so-called "military-industrial complex" point to this integration. The complex process of bringing gasoline to market, a far less controversial matter, illustrates the ways in which both private and public organizations necessarily coordinate and integrate activities:

> An oil operator brings oil to the surface of the ground; the local government prevents the theft of oil or the destruction of equipment; a railroad corporation transports the oil; State and Federal Governments prevent interference with the transport of oil; a refining company maintains an organization of workers and chemical equipment to convert the oil into more useful forms; a retail distributor parcels out the resulting gasoline in small quantities to individuals requiring it; the Federal Government supplies a dependable medium of exchange which allows the oil operator, the railroad, the refining company, and the retailer to act easily in an organized fashion without being under a single administrative authority, and enforces contracts so that organizing arrangements on specific points can be more

[5] Ibid., p. 15.

safely entered into; finally, government maintains a system of highways and byways which allow an ultimate consumer to combine the gasoline with other resources under his control in satisfying his desire for automobile travel.[6]

These rather innocuous cooperative endeavors are necessary in our complex society. They suggest, nevertheless, the manner in which government and private organizations work together in an integrated fashion to achieve common ends. More important, they are indicative of the interdependent and mutually supportive relationships which exist between bureautechnocratic systems.

Government participation in the activities of the marketplace are not limited to attempts at control or cooperative endeavors. Government is also an active participant in the economy. Galbraith has pointed out that "the services of Federal, state and local governments now account for between a fifth and a quarter of all economic activity. In 1929 it was about eight percent. This far exceeds the government share in such an avowedly socialist state as India, considerably exceeds that in the anciently social democratic kingdoms of Sweden and Norway, and is not wholly incommensurate with the share in Poland, a Communist country which, however, is heavily agricultural and which has left its agriculture in private ownership."[7]

If anyone avoids direct or indirect contact with bureautechnocracy as represented in the corporation, he does not escape contact with government. It employs millions of workers, pays us our Social Security, and demands taxes.

Our reasons for speaking of bureautechnocracy as an environment should now be clear. Business, leisure, education, politics, human drives and values: all these become the objects of bureautechnocratic attention and manipulation. In substituting

[6] U.S. National Resources Committee, *The Structure of the American Economy*, pt. 1, 1939; quoted in Harry S. Kariel, *The Decline of American Pluralism* (Stanford: Stanford University Press, 1961), pp. 17–18.
[7] Galbraith, *The New Industrial State*, p. 14.

bureautechnocracy for Ellul's *technique* we get the following picture of why today's citizen is integrated into and absorbed by bureautechnocracy:

> [Bureautechnocracy] requires predictability and, no less, exactness of prediction. It is necessary, then, that . . . [bureautechnocracy] prevail over the human being. For . . . [bureautechnocracy], this is a matter of life and death. . . . [Bureautechnocracy] must reduce man to a technical animal, the king of the slaves of . . . [bureautechnocracy]. Human caprice crumbles before this necessity; there can be no human autonomy in the face of technical autonomy. The individual must be fashioned by . . . [bureautechnocracy] either negatively (by the techniques of understanding man) or positively (by the adaptation of man to the technical framework), in order to wipe out the blots his personal determination introduces into the perfect design of the organization.[8]

Whether man is adapted to this environment through the negative or positive ways described above by Ellul, the fact is that he is adapting to a new environment. Bureautechnocracy, conceived as environment, is a sort of envelopment, a near-totality in which man is immersed.

> It is the ideal men usually have in mind when they speak of modernizing, updating, rationalizing, planning. Drawing upon such unquestionable imperatives as the demand for efficiency, for social security, for large-scale co-ordination of men and resources, for ever higher levels of affluence and ever more impressive manifestations of collective human power . . . [bureautechnocracy] works to knit together the anachronistic gaps and fissures of the industrial society. The meticulous systematization Adam Smith once celebrated in his well-known pin factory now extends to all areas of life, giving us human organization that matches the precision of our mechanistic or-

[8] Jacques Ellul, *The Technological Society*, trans. John Wilkinson (New York: Random House, 1964), p. 138.

ganization. So we arrive at the era of social engineering in which entrepreneurial talent broadens its province to orchestrate the total human context which surrounds the industrial complex.[9]

THE ORIGINS OF BUREAUTECHNOCRACY

It has been noted that bureautechnocracy is a system of organization and control born out of the confluence of bureaucratic structures and procedures, and standardized, rationalized means for achieving predetermined ends. Clearly this is not enough; it does not adequately explain the nature of bureautechnocracy. To know that John Doe is the child of Jane Smith and James Doe tells us little about John. When was he born? What was the nature of his childhood experiences? In short, to better understand the nature of bureautechnocracy we must know more about its background.

Bureautechnocracy is not a logical or natural codicil of our "national character" or philosophy of government. In fact, there is much in the American ethos (e.g., "rugged individualism," pluralistic philosophy, etc.) which contradicts bureautechnocracy and its products. Capitalism cannot be viewed as the major culprit either. Although our capitalistic economic system provides a milieu favorable to the growth and maintenance of bureautechnocracy, it alone cannot sustain a bureautechnocratic system and environment; we know that the pivotal features and insidious consequences of bureautechnocracy also prevail in communistic and avowedly socialistic states. Thus the *origins* of bureautechnocracy are not to be found, as such, in our political, social, or economic system. We must look elsewhere.

The change from relatively simple tools to power-driven machinery, from the small shop or factory of the nineteenth century to the vast industrial plants of today, from small-scale to mass

[9] Theodore Roszak, *The Making of a Counter Culture* (Garden City, N.Y.: Doubleday, 1969), pp. 5–6.

production provided the scenario within which bureaucracy and technology developed individually and then merged. It was during the early years of the so-called Industrial Revolution in which the successes of science and its methodology (the essence of technology) as they related to the workaday world made themselves apparent. The steam-driven engine and the electric light bulb were just two of the many scientific achievements which had significant impact in their application to the world of work. These successes stimulated intensive efforts in applying the findings of science and other organized knowledge to the work process. It was, however, the success of Henry Ford's assembly line which showed the world how rationalized procedures applied to management and production could increase production at reduced energy, time, and cost. Bureaucracy and technology now began what was to be a relatively short courtship. As pointed out by Kariel, "industrialization necessarily implied a systematic rationalization of the work process, a scrupulous effort to keep work from being anything more than a function of the finished product. The rigorous exclusion of irrationality—of whatever may be incalculable and unpunctual, irritating and shocking, subjective and ambiguous—was and is its logical imperative."[10]

The successful application of scientific and other organized knowledge to an increasingly organized and bureaucratized work process (such success measured primarily in terms of increased machine power, as opposed to manpower, and increased production and profit at reduced time, energy, and cost) has to be viewed as the single most important contributor to the growth of bureautechnocracy. Furthermore, the bureautechnocratization of the work process had important social and cultural consequences which promoted the growth of bureautechnocracy in areas outside of work per se.

"Historically, the mechanization of production engendered the familiar *shift from diffused small communities of workers to*

---

[10] Kariel, *Decline of American Pluralism*, p. 16.

concentrated large ones, from rural life to urban life, from agricultural pursuits to industrial ones—shifts that produced a new fourth estate of lonely and hence *community-seeking people.* Their old attachments to farms and villages were replaced by attachments to the new slots within the industrial order."[11] Large organized industries, large and increasingly complex urban centers, lonely community-seeking people—all these gave rise to conditions wherein bureautechnocratic systems of organization and control were deemed necessary and good for dealing with new and complex needs. Public and private agencies, copying the bureaucratic and technological procedures of industry, were established to serve the needs of rural and small-town refugees. These needs, ranging from basic health and welfare needs to those which issue from loneliness, were the target of numerous organizations, many endeavoring to ape the early successes of industrialization by copying their procedures. These far-ranging needs, and the consequent establishment of organizations to deal with them, were expanded and intensified by the influx of immigrants from abroad to the large urban centers. Bureautechnocracy as system, be it in government, industry, church, or school, was emerging at a time when social conditions were such that its services, procedures, etc., were deemed essential. However, the early success of bureautechnocracy in the world of work, and the establishment of the conditions favorable to an operational bureautechnocracy in the larger social arena, had to wait upon the successes achieved by the federal government in combating the social and economic ills engendered by the depression of the 1930's before it was to be established as an environment.

The alphabet agencies created by the Roosevelt administration were fine models of the way in which bureaucratic structures and rationalized procedures can be combined to tackle broad and complex social problems. The successful combination of these systems by the federal government in the 1930's intensified and extended the early successes of bureautechnocracy in

[11] Ibid. Italics ours.

the industrial process and in the many and varied agencies designed to handle the complexities of the growing urban centers. If bureaucracy and technology began the courtship process with the early work of Henry Ford and the bureaucratization of work, they certainly became engaged during the Depression years. And we might add, extending our metaphor, that they became married during World War II and have been on a honeymoon ever since!

This rather cursory and admittedly simplistic overview of the origins of bureautechnocracy is intended to show that, above all else, bureautechnocracy owes its existence and continued good health to the Industrial Revolution and the concomitant urbanization of the United States. This continuing revolution has made possible those environmental conditions conducive to the continued existence of bureautechnocracy, and the overt display of its apparent successes. More specifically, the continuing Industrial Revolution has stimulated population growth and the concentration of people in large urban cities; it has given rise to the huge industrial complexes of our day; it has intensified an economic system compatible with the expansive needs of bureautechnocracy; and it has contributed to the making of a society which is malleable and open to rapid bureautechnological changes and invention.

SOME CONSPICUOUS CONSEQUENCES

Perhaps the most obvious of bureautechnocracy's consequences is what Ellul (*The Technological Society*) calls the "process of massification": the creation of mass society. The characteristics of mass society have been discussed by many writers, and we are not interested, at this point, in reiterating what they have said. It should be recognized, however, that the term "mass society" refers to the fact that the cultural boundaries of our society have been or are being pushed out to a more common boundary in which all societal members participate. "Hundreds of millions of people can now participate in a single social system. They can keep in touch with one another. They can share wants, and they can share means for satisfying those wants."[12] These and other major features of mass society are commonly recognized and well understood. Less well understood, however, is the fact that modern man pays a great price for mass society.

> Previous societies took their character to a very large degree from the men in them. Technical or economic conditions imposed certain sociological structures, but the human being was in essential agreement with these structures, and the form society took expressed the psychology of the individual. This is no longer true. The process of massification takes place not because the man of today is by nature a mass man, but for technical reasons. Man becomes a mass man in the framework imposed upon him because he is unable to remain for very long at variance with his milieu.[13]

The imposition of a bureautechnocratic framework upon man demands, among other things, that man surrender a measure of individuality and self-realization, and that he repress those needs which speak of individuality. This adjustment has been well documented in regard to individuals within large organizations (e.g., William H. Whyte, *The Organization Man*). Such studies continually point out that, among other things, large organizations (bureautechnocratic *systems*) extract this adjustment by creating a system and environment which respects and rewards precisely those values, aspirations, skills, etc., that serve *system* needs. (The organization man must be a team worker. He must reflect a certain style of dress. He must be careful in his expression of political attitudes and ideas. Above all else, the goals of the organization stand above those of any individual.) Although

[12] Raymond W. Mack, *Transforming America: Patterns of Social Change* (New York: Random House, 1967), p. 106.
[13] Ellul, *The Technological Society*, pp. 332–33.

some excellent studies have focused on the large organization-like demands of mass society upon the individual, (e.g., David Riesman, *The Lonely Crowd*; Karen Horney, *The N rotic Personality of Our Time*; Jacques Ellul, *The Technological Society*), these have not been so readily accepted and well understood as those which focus on large organizations. Nevertheless, bureautechnocracy as *environment* operates in much the same way, making demands upon the individual which are similar to those of bureautechnocracy as *system* (the large organization).

In many ways, the drive and rapid movement which characterize our society and members of it are means of escape, ways of avoiding the realities of a repressive environment. This was Erich Fromm's major thesis in *Escape from Freedom*, and the whole notion has been summed up by Jules Henry in the following manner: "If you put together in one culture uncertainty and the scientific method, competitiveness and technical ingenuity, you get a strong new explosive compound . . . *technological drivenness*,"[14] a propelling force for constant expansion (in the name of progress) for society as a whole, and the motivating determinant for individual pain-free adjustment to the repressive demands of bureautechnocracy. "Technological drivenness," a function of the combined efforts of massive industrial growth and technical creativity, refers to the continual expansion and rapid change which characterize advanced industrial society. Technical creativity results in new discoveries and inventions. These result in new industries offering the new products which come from the discoveries and inventions. The demand for new products, however, must be created; this results in further industrial expansion. Such expansion could lead to the exhaustion of natural resources, so scientists and technologists are employed to find new ones. And the drive goes on.

Technological drivenness provides us with an outlet; it permits us to escape the realities of an oppressive environment. It

14 Jules Henry, *Culture against Man* (New York: Random House, 1963), p. 15.

affords us the means for escaping what our society professes and what it does. We profess attachment to an ethic which places high values on the individual and his inherent worth; we talk about brotherly love, cooperation, personal freedom, responsibility, and pluralism. Yet we have created a system whose norms stress the opposite. Norms such as competition, expansiveness, profit, aggressiveness, collective power, and group personality are far from brotherly love, human dignity, etc. "The disequiliberation between the traditional affirmation and the new . . . [norms] has produced the climate of anxiety and insecurity characteristic of our epoch and of our neuroses, and corresponds exactly to the distinction between the individualist society and the mass society."[15]

Repression can be an effective psychological escape mechanism, but continued repression can issue in mental illness. Henry has noted in this regard: "We are as highly developed in psychopathology as in technology."[16] (Bureautechnocracy, perhaps more than anything else, is helping to make psychiatry one of the most popular and lucrative of the medical specialties.) Anxiety, insecurity, etc., are best countered in a bureautechnocratic environment by repression of those needs not met by the system, and which accordingly give rise to anxiety in the first place. What we have, then, is a vicious circle. Our anxieties, which are often neuroses-producing, are avoided by repression which, in the long run, may very well issue in neuroses.

Moreover, bureautechnocracy insures its own existence and continued growth by inducing technological drivenness and by providing the means (material goods, increased services, increased standard of living, etc.) for repression. We find, paradoxically, escape in and through that which created the need for escape in the first place. Accordingly, we support by default the belief that bureautechnocracy is necessary and "good" for organizing and controlling a complex society.

15 Ellul, *The Technological Society*, p. 333.
16 Henry, *Culture against Man*, p. 322.

Indeed, as bureautechnocracy extends itself, it appears capable of absorbing everything into "its way of life." In his analysis of contemporary society Herbert Marcuse speaks of "repressive desublimation," namely, bureautechnocracy's ability to provide escape and satisfaction in such a way as to generate submission and absorb discontent. Theodore Roszak (*The Making of a Counter Culture*) puts it this way:

> The problem is sexuality, traditionally one of the most potent sources of civilized man's discontent. To liberate sexuality would be to create a society in which technocratic discipline would be impossible. But to thwart sexuality outright would create a widespread, explosive resentment that required constant policing; and, besides, this would associate the technocracy with various puritanical traditions that enlightened men cannot but regard as superstitious. The strategy chosen, therefore, is not harsh repression, but rather the *Playboy* version of total permissiveness which now imposes its image upon us in every slick movie and posh magazine that comes along. In the affluent society, we have sex and sex galore—or so we are to believe. But when we look more closely we see that this sybaritic promiscuity wears a special social coloring. It has been assimilated to an income level and social status available only to our well-heeled junior executives and the jet set. After all, what does it cost to rent these yachts full of nymphomaniacal young things in which our playboys sail off for orgiastic swimming parties in the Bahamas? *Real* sex, we are led to believe, is something that goes with the best scotch, twenty-seven dollar sunglasses, and platinum-tipped shoelaces. Anything less is a shabby substitute. Yes, there is permissiveness in the technocratic society; but it is only for the swingers and the big spenders. It is the reward that goes to reliable, politically safe henchmen of the status quo. Before our would-be playboy can be an assembly-line seducer, he must be a loyal employee.
>
> Moreover, *Playboy* sexuality is, ideally, casual, frolicsome, and vastly promiscuous. It is the anonymous sex of the harem.

It creates no binding loyalties, no personal attachments, no distractions from one's primary responsibilities—which are to the company, to one's career and social position, and to the system generally. The perfect playboy practices a career enveloped by noncommittal trivialities: there is no home, no family, no romance that divides the heart painfully. Life off the job exhausts itself in a constant run of imbecile affluence and impersonal orgasms.

Finally, as a neat little dividend, the ideal of the swinging life we find in *Playboy* gives a conception of femininity which is indistinguishable from social idiocy. The woman becomes a mere playmate, a submissive bunny, a mindless decoration. At a stroke, half the population is reduced to being the inconsequential entertainment of the technocracy's pampered elite.[17]

Bureautechnocracy has created conditions wherein it is difficult to be oneself. It is the "social man," the "other-directed" man, who is rewarded by bureautechnocracy.

The "social man" who lives up to the standards of his environment is also the "good man." For him to prove himself good he must show his attachment to society, its goals and methods: for society to show *its* goodness, it (its leaders and spokesmen) must demonstrate that people are attached to it and that it fulfills their aspirations. Once the individual's attachment to society is taken for granted (the anti-collectivist, the nonconformist, that is the *private man*, is not a political adversary but a heretic outside the sphere of unanimity), and once sociey rewards him by nursing him from cradle to grave, there is no need for *politics* which is the balancing of conflicts and interests: the dialogue between the good man and the good society is sufficient in itself and makes any other form of association and channel superfluous, even suspect.[18]

[17] Roszak, *The Making of a Counter Culture*, pp. 14–15.
[18] Thomas Molnar, *The Decline of the Intellectual* (New York: World Publishing, 1961), pp. 118–19.

The desire to live up to the standards of the environment does not just happen; people must be motivated to do so. Societal members must be made confident that the system is attached to them and will fulfill their needs and aspirations. Listen to the National Association of Manufacturers:

> For the expanding, dynamic economy of America, the sky is the limit. Now more than ever we must have confidence in America's capacity to grow. Guided by electronics, powered by atomic energy, geared to the smooth, effortless working of automation, the magic carpet of our free economy heads for distant and undreamed horizons. Just going along for the ride will be the biggest thrill on earth.[19]

. . . and the President of the United States:

> With all of our complaints, with all of our sufferings, our inconveniences, our setbacks, our frustrations, I think that all of us have good enough judgment to know that we are on the way, that we are moving, that we are getting bigger every day.[20]

Thus bureautechnocracy must communicate the content, the way of thinking—the cultural motif—of the system, so that it becomes embedded in the stable expectations of those who are members of it. More specifically, and as in the case of any bureaucratized organization, bureautechnocracy (as environment) through its representatives must define and elaborate a relatively stable set of mutual expectations. "This is what you can expect from the system. . . . This is what is expected of you." Sometimes these expectations are symbolic and inferred; an increase in the Gross National Product implies that the system is doing well and that we can expect increased prosperity and enjoyment of the "good life" if we do more of what we did to stimulate the increase.

---

[19] National Association of Manufacturers, *Calling All Jobs* (October, 1957): 21.

[20] President Lyndon B. Johnson, as quoted in *Time*, October 13, 1967.

Sometimes these expectations are confronted directly. The above excerpt from the President's speech suggests that disagreement with the statement is a sign of poor judgment. Any criterion of the efficiency and efficacy of bureautechnocracy, therefore, must be related to its ability to win the loyalty of its members, to convince them that the needs of the collectivity and the system are individual needs, and vice versa. The fact that ours is an age of deference to public opinion, collective security, mass tastes,[21] and "other-directedness" is evidence of the increasing success enjoyed by bureautechnocracy.

In winning people over through assimilation of needs and aspirations, i.e., through "massification," the self (however defined) becomes an organization of integrated behavior created, imposed upon, and manipulated by system needs. Bureautechnocracy socializes us into believing that the "real freedom of the individual consists in alienating . . . [individuality] for the benefit of the collectivity, which will guarantee for . . . [us as individuals] security among . . . the others."[22]

The priority of the collectivity over the individual is not necessarily unique to our society, nor is it a recent phenomenon. Alexis de Tocqueville, a Frenchman who visited the United States for a period of less than a year during 1832–33, wrote in his classic *Democracy in America*: "When I survey this countless multitude of beings, shaped in each other's likeness, among whom nothing rises and nothing falls, the sight of such universal uniformity saddens and chills me."[23] Any comment about contemporary collective priority or conformity pales in the light of this 137-year-old observation. There is, however, a uniqueness about the dominance of the collectivity today: it is consciously used by the representatives of bureautechnocracy (mass media, business, government, advertising) to shape individual thought.

---

[21] A sign outside a fashionable Chicago suburban restaurant unwittingly but proudly proclaims: "Our food and coffee is made to fit the United Tastes of America."

[22] Molnar, *The Decline of the Intellectual*, p. 120.

[23] Quoted in Henry, *Culture against Man*, p. 5.

Our tastes—in dress, TV programming, automobile style—are manufactured for us.

A more important difference is the *greater degree* of influence exerted by today's collectivity. This is evidenced in the declining or diminishing frames of reference from which an individual takes cues for his beliefs, attitudes, and behavior. In a society which is pluralistic and less collectivist dependent, an individual is in contact or is afforded the possibility of contact with individuals or groups whose patterns of value, behavior, etc., are in striking contrast with his own. There is a great deal of responsibility placed upon the individual in such a society, for it is not easy to interpret, translate, and synthesize the differing values into a pattern one must take as his own. In bureautechnocracy, the individuals and groups encountered in our daily lives are *increasingly similar* in values, behavior, and general life styles. This was not the case in the America about which Tocqueville was writing. In contemporary America, increasingly, "the individual's directive attitudes, *viz.*, ego attitudes, which define and regulate his behavior to other groups, and . . . to himself, are formed in relation to . . . [the prescriptions of bureautechnocracy]. They constitute an important basis of his self identity, [and] of his sense of belongingness."[24]

AN ARISTOCRACY OF POWER

The translation of individual into social needs and the corresponding emphasis on the collectivity suggest—theoretically—that a bureautechnocratic environment would be characterized by a diffusion of power. No individual or individual group would stand above the collectivity. Sanctions for beliefs and behavior would not be located in any one group or institution. In reality, however, bureautechnocracy breeds concentration in decision-making giving rise to an aristocracy of power. This

---

[24] M. Sherif, *Group Relations at the Crossroads* (New York: Harper and Row, 1953), p. 214.

elite is not as highly visible as power aristocracies are in states that are clearly fascist or totalitarian. Bureautechnocracy's aristocracy of power is camouflaged behind bureaucratic and technological complexes. Vance Packard refers to this aristocracy as the hidden persuaders. John Kenneth Galbraith calls it the technostructure, and Jules Henry refers to the individuals who make it up as cultural maximizers. Whatever the preferred label for this elite, it is comprised, essentially, of scientists, engineers, corporate executives, military leaders, advertising executives, political leaders, and show business personalities.

The emergence of a "power elite" in a society such as ours is not surprising, even though it would appear to conflict with our professed attachment to a democratic way of life. In bureautechnocracy,

> nothing is any longer small or simple or readily apparent to the nontechnical man. Instead, the scale and intricacy of all human activities—political, economic, cultural—transcends the competence of the amateurish citizen and inexorably demands the attention of specially trained experts. Further, around this central core of experts who deal with large-scale public necessities, there grows up a circle of subsidiary experts, who, battening on the general social prestige of technical skill in the technocracy, assume authoritative influence over even the most seemingly personal aspects of life: sexual behavior, child-rearing, mental health, recreation, etc. In the technocracy everything aspires to become purely technical, the subject of professional attention. The technocracy is therefore the regime of experts—or of those who can employ the experts. Among its key institutions we find the "think–tank," in which is housed a multi-billion-dollar brainstorming industry that seeks to anticipate and integrate into the social planning quite simply everything on the scene. Thus, even before the general public has become fully aware of new developments, the technocracy has doped them out and laid its plans for adopting or rejecting, promoting or disparaging.[25]

[25] Roszak, *The Making of a Counter Culture*, pp. 6–7.

Three features of this power elite demand attention. First of all, members of this group are offered the "chance to grow, to achieve recognition for performance as an individual—precisely what is denied most workers."[26] The elite is afforded recognition and reward for "job" efforts. Except for this group, most Americans are not emotionally involved with their work, and they find little opportunity for expression of and recognition of individuality. As Henry noted:

> The majority of workers—the factory hands, mechanics, laborers, truck drivers, minor clerical and sales workers, all those millions (61% of the labor force) engaged in routine work requiring little education or initiative—is concerned largely with raising their living standard and grasping for security (the worker drives). Competitiveness, profit, achievement, and expansion (the elite drives) belong more to scientists and other professionals, to corporation executives and managers—that is, to the elite and to their satellites and imitators. Few Americans, of course, are innocent of any one of these drives . . . it is in the latter group, however, that profit, achievement, expansion—the drives that maximize the culture—appear with greatest strength, are given the freest expression, and play over the most numerous areas of life.[27]

Swados, talking about factory workers, is more blunt:

> The plain truth is that factory work is degrading. It is degrading to any man who ever dreams of doing something worthwhile with his life; and it is about time we faced the fact. The more a man is exposed to middle class values, the more sophisticated he becomes and the more production line work is degrading to him. The immigrant who slaved in the poorly lighted, foul, vermin-ridden sweatshop found his work less degrading than the native-born high school graduate who reads "Judge Parker," "Rex Morgan, M.D.," and "Judd Saxon,

[26] Henry, *Culture against Man*, p. 32.
[27] Ibid., pp. 29–30.

Business Executive," in the funnies, and works in a flourescent factory with ticker-tape production control machines. For the immigrant laborer, even the one who did not dream of socialism, his long hours were going to buy him freedom. For the factory worker of . . . [today], his long hours are going to buy him commodities. . . .[28]

The second important feature of this power elite is the fact that the environment in which it exercises its power is such that the real needs of the people, as voiced and defined by the people, are paid little attention. Their exercise of power is therefore not genuinely social. There are several reasons for this.

In the first place the flow of communication, which is an instrument of power and which functions as a coordinating agent of people and processes within any system, comes from the "top," and policy is most often modified from the top only. However, information or communications from the "bottom" which may be crucial to qualitative policy modification seldom reach the top and have very little impact on policy change. A contemporary governmental policy may illustrate this problem. A part of the U.S. Department of Agriculture's food surplus program is designed to alleviate the problem of poverty. Our concern here is with that aspect of the program wherein persons who qualify are permitted to purchase food stamps. A given stamp may be purchased for X dollars, but the stamp will have the purchasing power of 2X or 3X. In some parts of the country, however, stamps can only be purchased in multiples of a given number of dollars —as much as $50 worth, or more, in some areas. Numerous people, including many who qualify for the food stamp program, have continually pointed out to the authorities that people living in poverty find it difficult to save any amount of money and that, therefore, the multiple dollar purchasing requirement defeats the aims of the program. Nevertheless, the food stamp program

---

[28] Harvey Swados, "The Myth of the Happy Worker," in M. Stein, A. J. Vidich, and D. Manning, eds., *Identity and Anxiety* (Glencoe, Ill.: The Free Press, 1960), p. 202.

continues to operate as is. Officials in the program answer their critics by claiming that overcoming this admitted program weakness would require changes so drastic that the program would very likely have to be completely overhauled. This is reason enough, claim those at the "top," for keeping the program as is! Automobile safety presents us with another illustration of the contrasocial exercise of power by the power elite. Since Ralph Nader's criticisms we have witnessed substantial progress in the very grave matter of automobile safety, but in spite of real safety needs, automobile manufacturers persist in doing all they can to forestall the production of a safer automobile. We are told that we "really don't want a safe automobile," that it would be "too expensive for the consumer." Some manufacturers cloud the issue by claiming that "what we need are safe drivers, not safe cars." All this is offered, in reality, in defense of established automobile manufacturing procedures and to safeguard monies spent on the drawing boards (where this year's unsafe car is being planned into obsolescence by another unsafe car) and on advertising for future products much like those already produced.

In addition to the problem of communication, those at the very top of the system's ladder (and, hence, at the top of the elite) are most often managers of too wide a variety of functions. Paradoxically, in an age of specialization we find that those who manage the specialists were themselves trained as specialists but are required to be generalists. Some sociologists call this "trained incapacity." Individuals who stand out as competent in special fields are lifted out of those fields of specialization and competency onto the level of power.

A third important feature of the power elite is that the standards by which they are guided are not humane or even personal standards. Persons in positions of power, who devise and improve (for example) the corporation's system of rules, who plan production, etc., are guided by system goals and implied values. This is not to say that they are viciously irresponsible, but the supreme standard or principle governing their decisions is the *successful perpetuation of the productive system through profit and corporate expansion.*

> They are most concerned with the self-sufficient goods of efficiency and economy. Their values are self-referential; their orientation is solely toward means and techniques. Their power, in other words is validated by their success, every failure calling simply for a more concerted exercise of power, not for any reconsideration of the ends toward which it is exercised. Thus, those who formulate the rules for the industrial apparatus are as divorced from ends as those who obey them.[29]

The fact that the power elite is as divorced from ends as those who obey them should not be too surprising. This is a direct function of a bureautechnocratic system which in becoming environment has somehow become supra-organic, that is, existing beyond and after man even though a product of man; a product of man's genius which has somehow come to reign over man and as such has become an end unto itself.

> It is the system that prescribes, and the constituency—managers, workers, consumers—that conforms. In the name of economical production, the various parts of society are induced to serve. Their progressive adjustment to the imposed rhythms of work is made mandatory, for the system must remain free from all disturbances. To assure the progressive realization of a stable rationality, all manifestations of entrepreneurship must be absorbed and neutralized. Conflicts must be reconciled. Decisions, which involve choices and hence risks of failure, must be emptied of their personal decisiveness: they must seem to emerge as spontaneous expressions of the system as a whole, or, less perfectly, as directives gently issuing from a network of committees. Whatever touches the industrial apparatus, whether from within or without, must be made friendly and manageable.[30]

[29] Kariel, *The Decline of American Pluralism,* pp. 22–23.
[30] Ibid., p. 19.

This last feature of the power elite reveals a disturbing quality found in all bureautechnocracy: instrumental values very often become terminal values. The governing rules of the system, the rationalized organizations which make up bureautechnocracy, the technologies which are so important and pervasive, the system (organizational) and environmental methods and procedures which prescribe official relationships among persons, processes, and things—all these, designed as means, turn into ends.

We have examined bureautechnocracy in terms of definition, origins, conspicuous consequences, and the elite leadership it generates. The grip of this anti-man culture suggests that man's "capacity to use his culture against himself may yet overtake man and destroy him while he works on his ultimate problem—learning to live with himself."[31] This suggests, in turn, that some changes in bureautechnocracy are necessary. Criticism necessary to precipitate constructive change, however, is no easy matter. One of the most far-reaching of bureautechnocracy's social effects is its cultivated resistance to social criticism. To an uncritical common sense, bureautechnocracy appears to be the apex of reason operating for the good of all social groups and interests. Why criticize a system which has provided us with an increased standard of living, better health care, greater educational opportunity, limitless services, etc.? We suggest some compelling reasons in the next two chapters.

[31] Henry, *Culture against Man*, p. 11.

CHAPTER 2

Homogenization: Bureautechnocratic Imperative

TYPES OF CONFORMITY

The paradox with which we introduced Chapter One must now be restated: bureautechnocracy gets bigger, wealthier, and better as it generates conditions which are destructive of human potential. In this chapter we will examine the most pervasive and dangerous of these conditions: *increased homogeneity and the loss of personal identity*. Much has been written about increasing homogeneity (uniformity in attitudes, values, tastes, behavior, etc.) in our society and the loss of personal identity which seems to follow. David Riesman's "inner-directed" and "other-directed" categories remind us how far things have gone. But the phenomenon needs still further analysis. For one thing, a distinction should be drawn among types of conformity.

A homogenized society is one characterized by *sociological conformity*. In such a society the individual may never perceive his choices, his values, his beliefs, and his way of life, as conforming. On the contrary, in a homogenized society the indi-

vidual will very likely look upon his life style, etc., as the objectively "good" and "right" way of life. He does not *experience*
conformity.

Most analyses of conformity fail to make a distinction between sociological and *psychological* (experienced) conformity.
Such analyses are most often supported by comparative studies
between the America of today and that of fifty or so years ago.
When we look back at the United States as it was fifty years ago,
it is relatively easy, and certainly understandable, to conclude
that ours *was* a heterogeneous culture, and that in comparison
today's is conformist. What we fail to recognize, however, is the
fact that when we look back to our earlier history we do so with
an all-encompassing view; we tend to look at and reflect upon
the country *as a whole*. What we see then is a country with a
pluralism of cultures represented in large cities, small cities and
towns, and rural communities, all as different from their counterpart political entities (city to city) as from differing political
entities (large city to small town). This blinds us to the fact that
an individual living during that period found his cultural horizons fixed by the geographical and social-psychological boundaries of his community, a community which was relatively
isolated from the people and cultures of neighboring as well as
distant communities. Accordingly, the individual encountered
and came to know only his community and its life style. This life
style received both institutional (church, school, government,
family, etc.) and ideological (political, religious, philosophical)
support. Individual attachment to and affirmation of this culture
was not perceived (by self or others) or experienced as conformity. (This was especially true of small city, small town, rural
America and, accordingly, for most Americans. Fifty years ago,
large city population comprised less than 25 percent of the total.) "The prevailing manners, morals and customs . . . were usually accepted without question. They provided the basis for the
sense of identity. They defined—not one way of life among

many—but *the* way of life, the right way."[1] Yesterday's conformity, therefore, was sociological conformity; it takes an outsider, a sociological observer, to see it.

Increasing homogeneity is taking place shortly after and during the period when the institutional and ideological supports for isolated pockets of relative homogeneity were and are breaking down. We have experienced the cultures of these different "pockets" through our travels and changes in residences. The culture of Hollywood has been brought into our living rooms and bedrooms via TV, and we have attended schools and colleges with children and young adults who come from any number of distinctly different isolated pockets of relative homogeneity. The institutional and ideological supports for any one style of life are weakened, devalued, undermined. Exposure to a broad spectrum of values, morals, mores, cultures, etc., gives rise to questions which shake the very foundation of those things which went into the support of what was perceived as *the* way of life.

The great majority in this country has not escaped this culture clash and the shock which often follows. Most of us have moved our places of residence several times within a few short years, and few of us have not been a part of the shift in population toward the urban areas. The phenomenon of conformity must be examined as movement from sociological conformity to contact with different cultures which leads to questioning about the "old ways." This sort of contact can make for greater pluralism. However, bureautechnocracy is pushing back the cultural horizons of the different cultures with which we have had, are having, and could have contact to a more common all-inclusive mass culture. Bureautechnocracy has made possible the very rapid interchange of persons, things, and ideas, inevitably leading to increased uniformity. Bureautechnocracy has effected this in many ways, but particularly through industrialization.

[1] Allen Wheelis, *The Quest for Identity* (New York: W. W. Norton, 1958), p. 92.

The application of science and technology to the economic process has made possible mass production of goods. Mass production is profitable because modern transportation makes mass distribution possible and modern techniques of communication help to create and sustain a mass market. This combination of mass production and mass consumption pushes out the boundaries of a society. Hundreds of millions of people can now participate in a single social system. They can keep in touch with one another. They can share wants, and they can share means for satisfying those wants.[2]

This pushing out of our sociocultural boundaries, as we all know, produces a kind of domestic "culture shock." Wheelis speaks to this problem:

Identity can survive major conflict provided the supporting framework of life is stable, but not when that framework is lost. One cannot exert leverage except from a fixed point. Putting one's shoulder to the wheel presupposes a patch of solid ground to stand on. Many persons these days find no firm footing; and if everything is open to question, no question can be answered. The past half century has encompassed enormous gains in understanding and mastery; but many of the old fixed points of reference have been lost, and have not been replaced.[3]

Twelve or thirteen years ago, when Wheelis was writing, it may have been appropriate to argue that the "old fixed points" were not being replaced. A bureautechnocratic "pushing out" of our cultural boundaries, however, is producing a mass culture which is providing replacements for the "old fixed points." And this push out to a more common inclusive culture came (and, of course, is still coming) at a time when feelings of alienation, anxiety, discontinuity, and identity crises prompt us to look for

[2] Raymond W. Mack, *Transforming America: Patterns of Social Change* (New York: Random House, 1967), p. 106.
[3] Wheelis, *The Quest for Identity*, pp. 19–20.

stability, continuity, durability. Yet this push out and our eager-
ness to adjust to it in our quest for the "fixed points" of life come
at a time when we know a great deal about ourselves.

> Modern man has become more perceptive to covert motiva-
> tions, in both himself and others. Areas of experience formerly
> disassociated from consciousness have become commonplace
> knowledge. Passivity, anxiety, disguised hostility, masochism,
> latent homosexuality—these are not new with the present
> generation; what is new is the greater awareness of them.[4]

This extended awareness has opened many doors to greater
understanding. We know a great deal about the impact of culture upon the individual. We know a great deal about the impact
of a pluralistic culture upon individuals. We know a great deal
about homogenized (sociologically conforming) culture's impact upon the individual. We know a great deal about the anxieties engendered through contact with values, beliefs, behavior,
and *cultures* which question or deny our own. We know a great
deal about our willingness to readily adopt bureautechnocracy,
to surrender to the assimilative pressures which are corollaries of
such an adoption. All of this greater knowledge has created
a situation wherein our choices are increasingly perceived by
us and others as conformist in nature. This is *psychological*
conformity.

> Conformity may not have changed in degree, but our aware-
> ness of it has increased, and this entails a change in quality.
> Formerly it was not experienced as conformity at all, but
> rather as adherence to principle. One did not "conform" to
> the right way of life; one rather "elected"—proudly and with
> "free" will—to be honorable and upright. These categories did
> not appear to be defined by mores, but by divine revelation or
> self-evident truth. Today conformity is experienced more

[4] Ibid., p. 20.

largely as such—namely as adherence to custom. The change detracts from self-esteem as well as from security.[5]

As the cultural horizons are increasingly pushed back to a common mass culture, it is likely that homogeneity with its concomitant patterns of mental and behavioral uniformity will become *the* way of life. This is clearly suggested in the ways through which bureautechnocracy generates homogeneity and what follows in terms of personal identity.

HOMOGENIZING THE MASSES

Bureautechnocracy builds up and sustains pressures for standardization and uniformity. We need not look very far to find such pressures: in mass production, advertising, corporate organization, education. Any college student who has tried to get a recorded final course grade changed because of error somewhere along the system line can testify to the way in which a bureautechnocratized institution deals with the individual; he is treated as a standardized object, not as a unique human being with unique problems. Any individual who has had problems with erroneous bills from large business corporations can testify to the fact that the standardized processes set up to deal with the problems of this sort almost preclude the possibility of solution if the customer's case is at all unique. The overriding aim of bureautechnocracy is the reduction of variables and the elimination of the unexpected and unpredictable; the major consequence is increased homogeneity.

Studies of group and/or institutional influence on individual behavior have shown that the greater the pressure toward uniformity and conformity and the greater the homogeneity of the group (or uniformity of the institution's "character") applying the pressure, the greater is the individual change toward uni-

5 Ibid., p. 92.

formity.[6] We know, for example, that group consensus regarding acceptable rules for behavior in any number of daily life activities is becoming more important and influential, and the coercive influences brought to bear upon the individual to conform to the rules are increasing in strength and number. It is becoming much more difficult for us to "refuse to go along." Attendance at college is a fine illustration. Many college students frankly admit that they have been "steam-rollered" into getting a college education. Other choices upon high school graduation, such as a full-time job, attendance at a trade school, or enlistment in military service, would have exposed them to criticism from peers, parents, relatives, teachers—too heavy to bear. Furthermore, they do not relish the idea of being identified by society at large as "uneducated" for want of a college degree. Fashion in dress is another example. How many persons believe it inane to purchase new clothes when the closet is overstocked with yesterday's—still in excellent condition—clothes? Millions, we suppose! Nevertheless, these same millions still buy the new clothes at each of the slightest fashion changes for fear of being one inch or one button behind the trend. Harold Hodgkinson is on target when he tells us that we are rapidly approaching the point where, in order for any human performance to be effective and met with acceptance, it must agree with the consensus which surrounds it.[7]

It is no longer the "inner man" who provides the framework and sanction for choices; it is the other man, the group. We go to college even when "inside" we know that we do not want to. We purchase a new wardrobe even when we know it to be inane. Our surrender to the demands for uniformity points to one of the most frightening aspects of a bureautechnocratic environment: its power to transform the very personalities of those who come in contact with it.

[6] See, for example, M. Sherif, *The Psychology of Social Norms* (New York: Harper Torchbooks, 1966).

[7] Harold L. Hodgkinson, *Education, Interaction, and Social Change* (Englewood Cliffs, N.J.: Prentice-Hall, 1967), p. 12.

The term "introjection" perhaps no longer describes the way in which the individual by himself reproduces and perpetuates the external controls exercised by his society. Introjection suggests a variety of relatively spontaneous processes by which a Self (Ego) transposes the "outer" into the "inner." Thus introjection implies the existence of an inner dimension distinguished from and even antagonistic to the external exigencies—an individual consciousness and an individual unconscious *apart from* public opinion and behavior. The idea of "inner freedom" here has its reality: it designates the private space in which man may become and remain "himself."

Today this private space has been invaded and whittled down by technological reality. Mass production and mass distribution claim the *entire* individual, and industrial psychology has long ceased to be confined to the factory. The manifold processes of introjection seem to be ossified in almost mechanical reactions. The result is not adjustment but *mimesis*: an immediate identification of the individual with *his* society and, through it, with the society as a whole.[8]

Here Marcuse suggests that the invasion of the inner self by the outside world of bureautechnocracy results in the transformation of personality through the virtual denial and, hence, loss of "self," "inner freedom," or "critical reason."[9] Mimesis is in operation when an individual refuses to be critical about his own needs apart from the needs of society at large, or when he auto-

[8] Herbert Marcuse, *One-Dimensional Man* (Boston: Beacon Press, 1964), p. 10.

[9] "Critical reason" is included purposely. Psychologists agree that "self" is not an object or thing, but a process best identified as that whereby experience is turned into knowledge. This process is usually referred to as intelligence, problem-solving, critical reasoning, etc. The process of introjection has generally been identified with the self as process, i.e., the use of critical reasoning in translating, interpreting, synthesizing, and internalizing the "outer world" into the "inner world" of the individual. If self is a process often identified as critical reasoning, which in turn is operational in and basic to introjection, then the rejection of the latter in favor of mimesis is a rejection of critical reason.

matically identifies as *his real* needs those which he sees in others.

The shaping of personality is the result of a process not unlike that which takes place whenever one is socialized into any organized social system. As we are socialized into the macrocosmic environment of bureautechnocracy, as in any organized system, we become sensitized to cues of the "proper" attitudes one should exhibit, the "proper" behavior in any given role, and, in general, the "picture" one should present of himself in any given situation. Cues tell us, in effect, which side of ourselves we should present. Sometimes referred to as *signs*, cues are sociocultural stimuli, and they vary in terms of strength and distinctiveness. In any given interpersonal situation we present only those aspects of our individuality which are relevant to the prescribed behavior patterns suggested through cues by the people and things around us. ("Should I have that second martini? I'll wait until Joe reaches for his and watch for the boss's reaction to Joe." "Should I relate my views on the New Left? I had better wait to see how these people react to my long hair!") The importance of a cue—i.e., its relative strength—in determining a given response depends upon those aspects of a cue-producing situation deemed important or unimportant by the individual or individuals sensitive to the cue. Where personal freedom prevails, and where pluralism and self-expression abound, cues are many, coming from numerous and varied sources and often presenting conflicting (though not always distinct) alternatives. Conversely, where such freedom is diminished, where pluralism is nonexistent or minimal and where self-expression is devalued, cues are fewer in number; they emanate from similar sources and do not present as many conflicting, indistinct alternatives. In short, as a society becomes more homogenized, behavioral and attitudinal cues are increasingly similar and the cue sources increasingly powerful and much more behaviorally and attitudinally deterministic.

The shift from individually based sanctions and responsibility for choice to a collective sanction and responsibility raises other difficulties. As Hodgkinson says:

> The environment in today's interdependent technological society is increasingly *other people*, and people make notoriously bad symbols, because the symbol is then merely a mirror image of its maker. This does not mean that we are influenced only by people and not by things, but it does mean that the things with which we surround ourselves are interpreted pragmatically, and these things tend to remind us of the pressures and demands of people. . . . Our objects remind us . . . of other selves, virtually identical to our own. As a consequence, we tend increasingly to take our cues from the possessions and behavior of others and not from a tradition providing meaningful symbolic structures which enable us to interpret present experiences *for ourselves*. This means that the contemporary person who does have a deep commitment to certain values will have difficulty in finding significant objects or symbols through which he can express his commitment.[10]

Several social theorists have suggested that ours is a valueless or normless society, a society characterized by anomie (a French word best translated as "without rules"). But even this early in our analysis it should be clear that bureautechnocracy is not without its norms, values, or rules. It "is driven . . . by . . . achievement, competition, profit, and mobility . . . and by the drives for security and a higher standard of living. Above all, it is driven by expansiveness."[11] Expansiveness, competition, profit, mobility, technical ingenuity—all these are bureautechnocracy's motivating determinants, and they affect all who live in our bureautechnocratic environment. The reality of mass culture and the fact that the great majority of people in this country are attached to it (we wouldn't have mass culture without majority attach-

[10] Harold L. Hodgkinson, *Education in Social and Cultural Perspectives* (Englewood Cliffs, N.J.: Prentice-Hall, 1962), pp. 115–16.
[11] Jules Henry, *Culture against Man* (New York: Random House, 1963), p. 13.

ment thereto) suggests that bureautechnocracy's values and norms are being assimilated and are much more powerful than the theorists of anomie would have us believe.

One of the major reasons (if not *the* reason) for bureautechnocracy's homogenizing power is the system's deliberate creation and manipulation of illusory or (as Marcuse calls them) "false needs." False needs are those which are imposed upon the individual as his own *real* needs when in fact they are system needs. "Most of the prevailing needs to relax, to have fun, to behave and consume in accordance with the advertisements, to love and hate what others love and hate, belong to this category of false needs."[12] To these we should add such glaring "needs" as the new car every year, new and "exciting" forms of entertainment, the electric toothbrush, the new wardrobe, the twenty-four-hour deodorant, ad infinitum.

The satisfaction of false needs serves three major functions. (1) People are kept happy. This is a logical and natural consequence of the bureautechnocratically instilled belief that satisfaction of these needs is tantamount to the surfeit of real and basic needs. (2) Bureautechnocracy is seen to be the best and most efficient method of social organization and control for a complex society: bureautechnocracy creates the needs; it alone offers the means to satisfy them. (3) The repressive features of bureautechnocracy become blurred. If people are kept happy, if they believe that their "happiness" is due to the system, then it logically follows that the ills or evils of the system are less easily detected. It is difficult to imagine the great poverty in our society if you are not impoverished, to conceive of poverty and misery in our midst if all the communicative media emphasize the "good life" as that which is commonplace. In short, the satisfaction of false needs reduces the risk of discontent.

The obvious target of criticism here is the advertising industry. However, this industry (with its penchant for propaganda, half-truths, and lies) can operate as it does only because it is a

---

[12] Marcuse, *One-Dimensional Man*, p. 5.

part of and serves a much larger system which necessitates the creation of false needs. The values and drives of bureautechnocracy (competition, profit, mobility, expansiveness) must be communicated in a saleable manner. This ability has paid off for the advertising industry. There has been a huge growth in "the apparatus of persuasion" associated with the relatively recent but massive growth of new saleable goods and new markets. The success of advertising in selling goods and services has earned it the status of a quasi science. Advertising as a "science" is a process based upon persuasion through propaganda, but dependent upon the behavioral and social sciences for determining effective persuasive techniques. The massive growth and the quasi-scientific status of advertising are rewards for serving bureautechnocracy well.

Advertising is necessary to bureautechnocracy for several reasons. First, advertising is a very effective way of transmitting to and instilling in people the values and drives of the system. It may be advertising's major function is to promote and sustain "technological drivenness."[13]

> The primary purpose of advertising technique is the creation of a certain way of life. And here it is much less important to convince the individual rationally than to implant in him a certain conception of life. The object offered for sale by the advertiser is naturally indispensable to the realization of this way of life. Now, objects advertised are all the result of the same technical progress and are all of identical type from a cultural point of view. Therefore, advertisements seeking to prove that these objects are indispensable refer to the same conception of the world, man, progress, ideals—in short, life.[14]

Television commercials clearly, and above all else, serve this purpose. The life style represented in most of the commercials

13 See Ch. 1, p. 18.
14 Jacques Ellul, *The Technological Society*, trans. John Wilkinson (New York: Random House, 1964), p. 406.

is made to appear common to all, or within easy reach of all. Airline commercials would make us believe that everyone travels to the land of sun and fun. Everyone smokes, and all smokers are either handsome and virile men or comely young women, each in the company of a person of the opposite sex with the same youthfulness, vigor, sexiness. Such commercials also represent this common life style as the "good life." Traveling to Florida, smoking cigarettes, etc., are always pictured as "good" and beautiful. Any surprise, then, to see a few ghetto rioters looting stores, arming themselves with the tangibles of the "good life": TV's, portable radios, clothes, furniture? If you are the brutalized object of society, literally a second-class citizen, why not grab *the* "good life" to which you're entitled?

The second major function of advertising is *to create needs*. These needs must correspond, however, to the needs of bureautechnocracy. "The initiative in deciding what is to be purchased comes not from the sovereign consumer. . . . Rather it comes from the great producing organization which reaches forward to control the markets that it is presumed to serve and, beyond, [through advertising] *to bend the customer to its needs*."[15] The implantation of a certain conception of life and the creation of needs necessary to that way of life are tied in directly with the third major function of advertising: mass production only works if there is mass consumption. To take the risks out of production, to insure mass consumption, it is necessary to create tastes which are fairly uniform. The logical consequence is increased homogeneity:

> Advertising must affect all people; or at least an overwhelming majority. Its goal is to persuade the masses to buy. It is therefore necessary to base advertising on general psychological laws, which must then be unilaterally developed by it. The inevitable consequence is the creation of the mass man. As

[15] John Kenneth Galbraith, *The New Industrial State* (New York: New American Library, 1967), p. 18. Italics ours.

advertising of the most varied products is concentrated, a new type of human being, precise and generalized, emerges.[16]

These three major functions are all generally related to the bureautechnocratic imperative of translating social and/or system needs into individual needs, and vice versa. However, this translation is becoming so effective that we tend to forget or overlook the fact that "the only needs that have an unqualified claim for satisfaction are the vital ones—nourishment, clothing, lodging at the attainable level of culture. The satisfaction of these needs is the prerequisite for the realization of *all* needs, of the unsublimated as well as the sublimated ones."[17] We seldom reflect on the fact that we spend more money on our automobiles than on our children's education. We build one bomber that costs millions of dollars, but fight to the teeth any taxation which may serve to feed the millions in our country who go to bed hungry every night. We race to the moon (few of us will deny the excitement and thrill we felt when Armstrong and Aldrin set foot on the moon) while millions of Americans are racing to illness and death through poverty. The propagandizing for technological drivenness, the deliberate creation and manipulation of false needs, and the creation of an increasingly homogenized society and culture, all necessary to bureautechnocracy, are increasingly blinding us to the needs of man as man. "The very efficiency of [bureautechnocracy] . . . in . . . the satisfaction of . . . external needs has resulted in the slighting of plans for the satisfaction of complex psychic needs. . . . [This] has made society a grim place to live in, and for the most part human society has been a place where, though man has survived physically, he has died emotionally."[18]

Why this harsh criticism of false need satisfaction? If bureautechnocracy stifles individuality, promotes sociological con-

16 Ellul, *The Technological Society*, p. 407.
17 Marcuse, *One-Dimensional Man*, p. 5.
18 Henry, *Culture against Man*, p. 12.

formity, limits individual responsibility, and is destructive of human potential, why not let us take refuge in false need satisfaction? At least we have some psychological gain! Vance Packard (*The Status Seekers*) touches on this:

> The marketers, by promoting status striving through the purchase of goods, are giving people the sense that they are getting ahead. This, at the lower levels, is largely a consumption gain. But should we deprive people who are stuck in their jobs of even this psychological satisfaction? If we cannot give them a fair chance at making their livelihood in a creative way that offers them the opportunities to advance, should we take away from them—to return to the Roman parallel—their circuses?[19]

A negative answer would imply that nothing can be done about the oppressive and repressive functions of bureautechnocracy. However, the basic issue is not one of depriving people of psychological satisfaction, but rather one of making society a place wherein repression does not become a way of life.

It is no wonder that writers discuss the death of ideology and speak of anomie and valuelessness. Bureautechnocracy blunts recognition of its repressive features:

> [It] assumes a position similar to that of the purely neutral umpire in an athletic contest. The umpire is normally the least obtrusive person on the scene. Why? Because we give our attention and passionate allegiance to the teams, who compete within the rules; we tend to ignore the man who stands above the contest and who simply interprets and enforces the rules. Yet, in a sense, the umpire is the most significant figure in the game, since he alone sets the limits and goals of the competition and judges the contenders.[20]

[19] Vance Packard, *The Status Seekers* (New York: Pocket Books, 1959), p. 280.

[20] Theodore Roszak, *The Making of a Counter Culture* (Garden City, N.Y.: Doubleday, 1969), p. 8.

We must make ourselves aware of the repressive functions of bureautechnocracy and discover those tools which will help us to distinguish between real and false needs. What are real needs? "In the last analysis, the question of what are true and false needs must be answered by the individuals themselves, but only the last analysis; this is, if and when they are free to give their own answer."[21] When will individuals be free to give their own answers? This is a difficult question to answer; some possibilities are discussed in Chapters Seven and Eight. However, we do know that the deliberate creation and manipulation of false needs

> have a societal content and function . . . determined by external powers over which the individual has no control. . . . No matter how much such needs may have become the individual's own, reproduced and fortified by the conditions of his existence, no matter how much he identifies himself with them and finds himself in their satisfaction, they continue to be what they were from the beginning—products of a society whose dominant interest demands repression.[22]

The consequences of the three major functions served by false need satisfaction (people are kept happy, bureautechnocracy is seen as the best method of social organization and control for a complex society, the repressive features of the system become blurred) is the delivery of the individual over to the mass culture. Sociologists who have studied this phenomenon on a microcosmic level call it "identity management." The function of this process is to minimize or eliminate those qualities of personal identity which were important to an individual previous to induction into a given social system. After a period of time, the inductee tends to identify with the identity model provided by the system. This type of identity management is perhaps best exemplified by military training but takes place in corporations,

[21] Marcuse, *One-Dimensional Man*, p. 6.
[22] Ibid., p. 5.

fraternal organizations (think about fraternities and sororities), and professional organizations. In each of these instances the "individual is never envisaged as the locus of an internal autonomy, but rather as a chip from the block of collectivity, which possesses no other ingredient than what the block itself has in its makeup."[23] As our society becomes increasingly homogenized, and as collective security and deference to public opinion increasingly become the sanctions for individual behavior, we give more and more of ourselves over to bureautechnocratic identity management. We increasingly renounce introjection and critical reason (self) and turn to mimesis. We forsake those values which had been related to our personal identity in the past and automatically identify with values and drives (competition, profit, increased standard of living, mobility, expansiveness, etc.) which comprise the essence of a bureautechnocratic environment. Collective security, deference to public opinion, increased homogeneity, lack of individual responsibility, and the renunciation of self result in the diminution of individual freedom. This is not always clear; looking about, we may see an apparently wider range of choice today than ever before—a greater range of choice in material goods and services, in educational and vocational opportunity. And there appears to be greater opportunity and choice for self-expression in style of dress, for instance, a wider latitude of "non-mainstream" thought and action. However, this can stand analysis.

(1) There is little doubt that there appears to be a wider range of choice in goods and services than ever before, and that choice is a fundamental feature of pluralism and personal freedom. But an increased range of choice in these areas is a logical consequence of a system whose needs demand the continual creation of needs among members of society, needs which can be satisfied only through the consumption of newer and more goods and services. Bureautechnocracy needs people who want

[23] Thomas Molnar, *The Decline of the Intellectual* (New York: World Publishing, 1961), p. 215.

to consume more and more. The fact that I have a wider range of goods and services from which to choose in order to satisfy a consumption urge does not constitute freedom of choice if that urge has been manufactured, and imposed upon me, by agencies external to me.

Increased opportunity and a wider range of choice in terms of education and training are, like false needs, created by and for the system. Education is now the means for obtaining a "union card," that is, entry into the world of work. We do not value education in this country; we only value what an education can purchase. The fact that I can select among 100 different colleges to earn my B.A. degree does not make my choice more free if I must get a B.A. to hold down a job that requires a B.A. for functional, attractive reasons only. We require high school diplomas, junior college degrees, and college degrees for jobs which by any criterion other than bureautechnocratic need do not require much, if any, formal education. When we make education compulsory, it is contradictory to talk about freedom of choice in education. When we extend compulsory education upward to keep people out of the labor market as long as possible, it is inane to talk about greater choice in education. The *range* of choice is not the major criterion of freedom of choice, but *what* can be chosen and what *is* chosen by the individual."[24] In our increasingly homogenized society, choice is largely a determinant of the system and its needs.

(2) The new "freedoms" we experience in matters of dress and expression of "non-mainstream" thought are cited by many writers as evidence of greater choice, hence freedom. Even the most doctrinaire of these writers might agree, however, that choices in these areas do not *prove* the existence of greater freedom. The fact that one can speak lovingly of the Viet Cong while damning Richard Nixon does not mean that greater freedom is a condition of contemporary life. In point of fact, the new "freedoms" in this category can be viewed as evidence of a desire to

[24] Marcuse, *One-Dimensional Man*, p. 7.

be free *from* something. Diversity in dress styles, long hair and beards for the men, necklaces with peace symbols for everybody, etc., may say "I want to be free," rather than "I am free." In contemporary society these new "freedoms" are, most likely, mild forms of protest which express the desire to be free from the compelling forces of uniformity, to be free from economic forces and relationships, to be free from boring jobs, and to be free from politics over which individuals feel no control.

In many ways the new "freedoms" in this category serve the same purpose as false needs; they raise the threshold of psychic pain by allowing us to "let off steam." These new freedoms are, therefore, functional. They do not, largely, threaten the internal fabric of the system. When they do, the powers of bureautechnocracy show themselves. What happened to the hippies? What happened to the Poor People's Campaign?

> The reign of a one-dimensional reality does not mean that . . . the spiritual, metaphysical, and bohemian occupations are petering out. On the contrary, there is a great deal of "Worship together this week," "Why not try God," Zen, existentialism, and beat ways of life, etc. But such modes of protest and transcendence are no longer contradictory to the status quo and no longer negative. They are rather the ceremonial . . . [consequences of bureautechnocracy,] its harmless negation, and are quickly digested by the status quo as part of its healthy diet.[25]

In addition to the above, the very existence of "non-mainstream" ideas is evidence in support of the homogenization and diminished freedom theses. After all, many if not most of these are ideas which call for greater pluralism, greater freedom of choice, more involvement of the people in the political process, more meaningful jobs. Those who would cite the new "freedoms" of expression as indices of greater *choice*, hence freedom, must remember that they bespeak freedom only when they are cou-

25 Ibid., p. 14.

pled with the "existence of a social order which offers the individual a broad spectrum of diverse, independent, and poweful groups among which he can choose."[26] Recent social developments which appear to be evidence of greater choice are merely harmless ways of repressing and/or protesting the consequences of a bureautechnocratic environment—when we take them as proof of greater choice and freedom, we are acting in a manner appropriate to system needs. The reality of these developments is deceptive. "It seems to extend rather than reduce manipulation and coordination, to promote rather than counteract the fateful integration."[27] And this is a danger which is becoming much more difficult to combat because, as Marcuse has noted,

> we are immediately confronted with the fact that advanced industrial society becomes richer, bigger, and better as it perpetuates the danger. The defense structure makes life easier for a greater number of people and extends man's mastery of nature. Under these circumstances, our mass media have little difficulty in selling particular interests as those of all sensible men. The political needs of society become individual needs and aspirations, their satisfaction promotes business and the commonweal, and the whole appears to be the very embodiment of Reason.[28]

It is true that we have more choices than ever before. But we should remember that "free choice among a wide variety of goods and services does not signify freedom if these goods and services sustain . . . alienation. And the spontaneous reproduction of superimposed needs by the individual does not establish autonomy; it only testifies to the efficacy of the controls."[29]

We have a cultural disease which is eating at the very roots of

26 Charles Frankel, *The Democratic Prospect* (New York: Harper Colophon Books, 1962), p. 23.
27 Marcuse, *One-Dimensional Man*, p. 51.
28 Ibid., p. ix.
29 Ibid., p. 7–8.

human freedom: man's ability to choose knowingly and assume responsibility for his choice. Bureautechnocracy sets the limits of choice (at the same time encouraging the individual to believe that he exercises significant options) by defining the needs of the system as the needs of the individual. Bureautechnocracy must do this in order to sustain itself and in so doing must promote some sort of consensus or collective agreement on needs, interests, aspirations, moral convictions, political, religious, and spiritual beliefs, literature, entertainment, and so on. Consensus is further promoted by discrediting individual action and thought and by emphasizing their difference and social irrelevance.[30] This might be better understood through the famous analogy of the beehive.

THE ANALOGY OF THE BEEHIVE

The mode of existence for the individual in contemporary society is in several ways increasingly approximating that of the bee in the hive. The following conditions which exist in a beehive are not unlike those found in our society:

(1) *Complete division of activity by function.* Worker bees do certain things, drones do others. Activities of each (within and without the beehive) are determined by their functions. Intergroup and interpersonal relationships are conditioned by functional duties. In our society, specialization is the keynote of our time; it pervades most of our activities and circumscribes our interpersonal relationship.

(2) *Rationally organized hierarchy.* The roles of the various bee groups are functionally related to the colony—to make honey. Roles and their functional importance to the colony result in a rationally organized pecking order with

---

[30] Molnar, *The Decline of the Intellectual,* p. 214.

the queen at the top. In our society, bureautechnocratization has necessarily resulted in an ever increasing rationalized productive system. Roles and their functional importance to the system produce a hierarchy (management and labor, for example) with the power elite at the top.

(3) *Subordination of the individual to the needs of the system.* This is certainly the case in the beehive. The bee which gets "out of hand" is punished in any number of ways including death. We have hopefully made clear, vis-à-vis false needs, that in bureautechnocracy the individual is subordinate to system needs.

Functional division of labor, rational techniques of control and organization, system-circumscribed interpersonal relations, and the secondary importance of the individual—these fit bureautechnocracy as well as the beehive colony. Self-expression, individual differences, and unique needs are devalued. "Not all worker bees are *exactly* alike, but these differences are of no use to the collectivity and are therefore ignored."[31] If a bee persists in flaunting his uniqueness, he loses place in the colony and may be exiled or even killed by his fellow workers. We in bureautechnocracy have been known to do as much to our fellow man. We "force" hippies to colonize in a Haight-Ashbury: we demand that our male students remove their long sideburns or we dismiss them from high school; and we dismiss as "kooky" individuals and groups which question our national priorities.

There are several advantages to the beehive system not unlike those of a bureautechnocratic system. These advantages include efficient use of member energies, high capacity for work and orderliness, high capacity for production, little role confusion, and relative ease in manageability. This last "advantage" is particularly important to any rationally organized system. It follows principally from the fact that within bureautechnocracy

[31] Hodgkinson, *Education, Interaction, and Social Change*, p. 27.

the individual does not need an overall view of the system—its processes, goals, etc.—in order to function effectively.

> While technology ultimately unifies a fragmented industrial society, the individual is attached to only one part of the whole, and only dimly grasps how his part fits. He knows of his dependency but finds the order upon which he depends unintelligible. However rational the total process of production may be, from this rationality he is alienated; barely able to perceive it, he has no personal attachment to it. On his own, he is unlikely to develop a comprehensive view, and even if he does, it will probably take the form of an off-duty philosophy unrelated to his work. Whatever his role—even his role as a consumer of products—it tends to absorb him, to sap his humanity and creativity. He is displaced and pacified by a system which cannot permit him to take the initiative. There is no end—at least no end in clear sight—to his participation in the work process, for there is no objective other than the maintenance of the process itself.
>
> This perspective is not only relevant to the passive assembly-line worker. Managers, too, can be seen as little more than functions of a bureaucracy; owners can be seen as inactive recipients of income from property which is not meaningfully theirs; consumers can be seen as unreflecting purchasers whose market calculations are socially determined.[32]

In short, our roles—whatever they may be—are so system bound (in a specialized, functional way) and so all consuming that we have neither the capability, the need, nor the inclination to get a total perspective, an overall view of the system processes and goals. This accounts, largely, for the relative ease with which individuals in bureautechnocracy (or the beehive) are managed. This is illustrated at the macrocosmic level in the fact that as our society becomes increasingly complex, and ordered along the lines of bureautechnocracy, we as individual citizens find

[32] Harry S. Kariel, *The Decline of American Pluralism* (Stanford: Stanford University Press, 1961), pp. 17–18.

little difficulty in explaining away our failure to participate in (for example) the political process. How many of us can name the congressional representatives from our districts? Our state representatives? How many of us think it makes any difference? At a lower level we can cite the role of an inspector in a factory. His job is to inspect a product and to make sure that it meets specifications. His tenure is based on his ability to spot defective products. Success is determined on this ability, and the incumbent of such a role does not need to know much, if anything, about management of his factory or the way it relates to the outside world to maintain his job. Teachers or students in any large university or school system know that this also holds true for them.

As long as members of a system are ignorant of the system's overall perspective and goals, then they are relatively easy to manage. Freedom from servitude demands awareness of servitude. Freedom from manageability demands awareness of manageability. Bureautechnocracy is organized in such a way as to diminish or divert awareness, hence, the likelihood of increased manageability:

> So subtle and so well rationalized have the arts of technocratic domination become in our advanced industrial societies that even those in the state and/or corporate structure who dominate our lives must find it impossible to conceive of themselves as the agents of a totalitarian control. Rather, they easily see themselves as the conscientious managers of a munificent social system which is, by the very fact of its broadcast affluence, incompatible with any form of exploitation. At worst, the system may contain some distributive inefficiencies. But these are bound to be repaired . . . in time.[33]

The lack of necessity for total perspective is related to, and a logical consequence of, another major feature of bureautech-

---

[33] Roszak, *The Making of a Counter Culture*, p. 9.

nocracy: the importance of specialty, function, or role over that of person. Bureautechnocracy standardizes systems and processes, and generates a churchdom of specialized positions or roles, each with well-defined statuses and obligations which are functionally interdependent. (Think of the typical organization chart with its squares and lines depicting the relationship, responsibilities, statuses, and operational flow between organizational roles). Crucial to the standardized systems are the specialties called for in any given role; the specialty is more crucial than the person. More specifically, a specialty, not a person, occupies a particular role. An individual occupying a given role accepts the status and obligation called for, but he does not, as a person, become identical with the role itself; his specialty does. There is, therefore, a separation between the position and its incumbent.

There are two very important consequences of this separation of person from position. First of all, those individuals who are at the top of the system's hierarchy—the "cultural maximizers" (Jules Henry) or the power elite—come to have a vested interest in keeping the operation at a status quo.[34] As we noted in Chapter One, members of this group are rewarded by the system. They, unlike most in this country, have the opportunity to become *personally* involved with their work and to achieve recognition for their individual contributions. Furthermore, they exercise power over those who are more easily managed due to a system which demands separation of person from work. Members of the power elite do not, necessarily, perceive themselves as exercising totalitarian control nor preserving the status quo. But "the distinctive feature of the regime of experts lies in the fact that, while possessing ample power to coerce, it prefers to charm conformity from us by exploiting our deep-seated commitment to the scientific world-view and by manipulating the securities

[34] See Robert Merton's discussion of this as it relates to system means becoming ends; in *Social Theory and Social Structure.*

and creature comforts of the industrial affluence which science has given us."[35]

Second, and much more important, the separation of *person* from job (role, position, office) accounts largely for the wide-spread lack of involvement with work, a phenomenon which is diffused throughout our society. "Why put my *self* into my job when by definition my self is not called for?" Paradoxically, non-involvement with our work prepares us for placing trust in bu-reautechnocracy. If we cannot find meaning in our work, then give us something else! Let us satisfy our false needs and thereby gain at least some satisfaction!

> Since we require of most people that they be *un*involved in the institution for which they work, it follows that the ability to be uninvolved is a desirable quality in the American character. Meanwhile, since loyal workers are valued because every re-placement cuts into profits, we have a paradoxical situation in which, since *un*involvement—"What do *you* give a damn, bub?"—is valued also, loyalty is obtained through higher wages, fringe benefits, and seniority. This emotionless con-nection that finally pins a worker to his job is called "attach-ment" in the ambiguous language of labor economics.[36]

The demand for noninvolvement with work, the deliberate creation and manipulation of false needs, and the bureautech-nological imperative for homogeneity are all functionally related to the needs of bureautechnocracy. Taken together, these "func-tional requirements" have occasioned a shift in the authority by which persons sanction their beliefs and behavior. We increas-ingly approve attitudes and behavior which, as individuals, we might otherwise condemn. We let the system, rather than our own conscience, lay down the moral law.

Bureautechnocracy as environment is a very recent phenom-

---

[35] Roszak, *The Making of a Counter Culture*, p. 9.
[36] Henry, *Culture against Man*, p. 28.

enon, and most of us therefore were born and raised during a period in our history when this unique combination of bureaucracy and technology was just emerging and hardly felt. Accordingly, bureautechnocracy must reeducate us, acculturate us into its ways. In order to be successful in this regard it must, among other things, break down "old" beliefs, attitudes, values, and especially what Jules Henry called "old impulse controls."

THE REORDERING OF SUPER EGO

In the Freudian scheme of man's mental apparatus the term *Id* is used to refer to man's impulsive drives, cravings for pleasure, and immediate satisfaction of any felt need. *Super Ego* is the term used by Freud to represent the repository of ideas, values, mores, moral codes, etc., which acts as a brake on the impulses of the Id. In a general sense, Super Ego is synonymous with what we recognize as conscience. *Ego* is that part of man's mental apparatus which represents critical reasoning; it "hears" the conflicting demands of Id and Super Ego and decides, critically, the relative worth of such demands. We have already discussed bureautechnocracy's impact upon Ego or critical reasoning,[37] but in many ways it is this environment's impact upon the Super Ego which accounts for the shift in authoritative sanctions just discussed.

In order to break down old impulse controls, bureautechnocracy must replace or eliminate "Super Ego ideas" which would restrict certain impulses crucial to the satisfaction of false needs. For example, the traditional notion of forsaking immediate needs for more distant or long-range goals is not consistent with the needs of bureautechnocracy. Buying on credit, self-indulgence in food, clothes, or gadgets, conspicuous consumption—all these are necessary to bureautechnocracy but are anathema to the traditional Super Ego notion of forsaking immediate need satis-

[37] See discussion of mimesis, p. 38.

faction. Accordingly, bureautechnocracy must set out to break down this "traditional" idea. It does this in several ways, including the use of the advertising industry. In some cases the system operates in such a fashion as to make it virtually impossible for an individual to maintain a traditional repository of impulse controls. An acquaintance of one of the authors decided to buy a house in a suburb of a large midwestern city. This individual had been raised in a home and community where credit buying was frowned upon. He carried this tradition with him and was proud of the fact that he had no outstanding bills and carried only one credit card, that of a gasoline company. After finding a house that both he and his family liked, this individual applied for a home mortgage loan. When the potential lender discovered that this fellow had no open charge accounts other than with the gasoline company, he refused the loan until the fellow had established "credit" by opening and paying off some charge accounts. The only way this individual could get a loan from this mortgage house was, in effect, to forsake some of his beliefs about credit buying—in other words, to reorder or reject his Super Ego. In the case of this individual, as well as for most of us in bureautechnocracy, the reordering of Super Ego facilitates impulse release and "frees" us to satisfy the false needs[38] which are created by, and so necessary to, the existence and growth of a bureautechnocratic environment.

A pluralistic society suggests, by definition, involvement, personal responsibility, and the exercise of a Super Ego that has matured through encounter with difference—difference which does not make it impossible to personally identify with Super Ego–held ideas. Bureautechnocracy demands the opposite, and weakens Super Ego. The Super Ego moreover can constitute a major barrier to change.

[38] We are not suggesting in our illustration that purchasing a home is necessarily the satisfaction of some false need. It merely illustrates one way in which our system goes about breaking down old "impulse controls."

A society in which the prevailing social character is marked by a superego with authority of wide scope will offer relatively vigorous institutional opposition to technological change; and, conversely, a society in which the prevailing social character is marked by a superego with authority of diminished scope will offer diminished . . . opposition to technological change.[39]

This statement tells us two significant things about our society. First of all it suggests why the reordering of Super Ego is so necessary to bureautechnocracy. The productive, economic, organizational, and control aspects of this system rely on technology and rapid technological change. Second, this statement suggests that a decline in the traditional function of Super Ego, or a reordering of it, is symptomatic of the success of a bureautechnocratic system; i.e., we can infer that the system—while seemingly meeting the real needs of individuals—is meeting its own needs. Thus the "ideal" system comes to replace the "ideal" individual. The system's logic becomes the "good" logic. And we come to this:

We call it "education," the "life of the mind," the "pursuit of the truth." But it is a matter of machine-tooling the young to the needs of our various baroque bureaucracies: corporate, governmental, military, trade union, educational.

We call it "free enterprise." But it is a vastly restrictive system of oligopolistic market manipulation, tied by institutionalized corruption to the greatest munitions boondoggle in history and dedicated to infantilizing the public by turning it into a herd of compulsive consumers.

We call it "creative leisure": finger painting and ceramics in the university extension, tropic holidays, grand athletic excursions to the far mountains and the sunny beaches of the earth. But it is, like our sexual longings, an expensive adjunct of careerist high-achievement: the prize that goes to the dependable hireling.

[39] Wheelis, *The Quest for Identity*, p. 99.

We call it "pluralism." But it is a matter of the public authorities solemnly affirming everybody's right to his own opinion as an excuse for ignoring anybody's troubling challenge. In such a pluralism, critical viewpoints become mere private prayers offered at the altar of an inconsequential conception of free speech.

We call it "democracy." But it is a matter of public opinion polling in which a "random sample" is asked to nod or wag the head in response to a set of prefabricated alternatives usually related to the *faits accompli* of decision makers, who can always construe the polls to serve their own ends. Thus, if 80 percent think it is a "mistake" that we ever "went into" Vietnam, but 51 percent think we would "lose prestige" if we "pulled out now," then the "people" have been "consulted" and the war goes on with their "approval."

We call it "debate." But it is a matter of arranging staged encounters between equally noncommittal candidates neatly tailored to fit thirty minutes of prime network time, the object of the exercise being to establish an "image" of competence. If there are interrogators present, they have been handpicked and their questions rehearsed.[40]

NEUTRALIZATION OF COMPETING FORCES

There exist—at the large societal level—two forces which by nature would militate against homogeneity. These two forces are: (1) the competitive interests of partisan politics, and (2) the contradictory forces of labor and management. One could argue that the neutralization or destruction of the contradictory interests of the different groups in each of these two areas would topple any lasting and effective barrier to homogenization. This neutralization–destructive process evidences itself in the realm of domestic and foreign affairs. In foreign policy, bipartisanship is emphasized against competitive political interests under the

[40] Roszak, *The Making of a Counter Culture*, pp. 16–17.

threat of what is identified as an international, monolithic form of communism. We see it also in domestic policy where the two major parties use a different rhetoric—in order to attract interest and support—but mean virtually the same thing. Nixon called for law and order with justice; Humphrey called for justice with law and order. In this sense, bureautechnocracy

> eludes all traditional political categories. Indeed, it is characteristic of . . . [bureautechnocracy] to render itself ideologically invisible. Its assumptions about reality and its values become as unobtrusively pervasive as the air we breathe. While daily political argument continues . . . [bureautechnocracy] increases and consolidates it power . . . as a transpolitical phenomenon following the dictates of industrial efficiency, rationality and necessity. . . . The angry debates of conservative and liberal, radical and reactionary touch everything except . . . [bureautechnocracy], because . . . [it] is not generally perceived as a political phenomenon in our advanced industrial societies. It holds the place, rather, of a grand cultural imperative which is beyond question, beyond discussion.[41]

This neutralization process is also evidenced in the increasing similarity of, and fusion of, business and labor interests. The labor movement has historically been at odds with the needs and interests of business. The labor movement could be relied upon for stimulating qualitative change in our society. However, matters have dramatically changed. In seeking to come to grips with bureautechnocracy, labor has chosen to work with the existing system and has thereby reinforced it. Kariel put it this way:

> In a society whose workers . . . [have] overwhelmingly accepted the proposition that the business of America is business, a class conscious labor point of view . . . [can] become neither emphatic nor clear. However much resistance there has ac-

[41] Ibid., pp. 8–9.

tually been to the creed of the businessman, it has been so sporadic and isolated as to be unable to overcome a gradual blurring of the distinction between labor and business.[42]

David J. McDonald, addressing the American Management Association in 1956 as head of the United Steel Workers, told us then that this neutralization process is a natural and logical development given our "American way of life":

> After all, union leaders and company executives are trustees. We have it within our power to build our great enterprises, not only in size and volume but in service—service to the economy, service to the worker, service to the housewife and the family. We can do much to make life easier, better, more enjoyable, safer, healthier—for the people, giving them peace of mind and confidence . . . .
> The recognition that we each have a role to play and that together we can progress is the key to future prosperity. This mutual acceptance and knowledge of our trust is what I mean by "Mutual trusteeship." It is a logical expression of our American way and our progressive traditions.[43]

The absorption of labor into bureautechnocracy thus neutralizes a major barrier to increasing homogeneity.[44] The neutralization has, indeed, contributed directly to and made possible greater homogeneity!

> What has happened is that the union has become almost indistinguishable in *its own eyes* from the corporation. We see the phenomenon today of unions and corporations *jointly* lobbying. The union is not going to be able to convince mis-

[42] Kariel, *The Decline of American Pluralism*, p. 61.
[43] Ibid.
[44] Marxists assumed that the alienation of labor would have as its consequence the estrangement of the laborers from the factory system culminating in revolution. Advanced industrialized society has quite successfully curtailed this type of consequence.

sile workers that the company they work for is a fink outfit when both the union and the corporation are out lobbying for bigger missile contracts and trying to get other defense industries into the area, or when they jointly appear before Congress and jointly ask that missiles instead of bombers should be built or bombs instead of missiles, depending on what contract they happen to hold.[45]

ESTRANGEMENT FROM SELF

Bureautechnocratic demands for uniformity, collective security, technological drivenness, noninvolvement, repression, and renunciation of individuality are generating conditions which make it difficult for the individual to discover and maintain a meaningful personal identity. Bureautechnocracy needs individuals who will find security in the collectivity, who want to consume more and more, and whose tastes and aspirations can be manipulated and standardized. "It needs men who feel free and independent, not subject to any authority, or principle, or conscience—yet willing to be commanded, to do what is expected, to fit into the social machine without friction."[46] In short, bureautechnocracy needs men who have been separated from themselves.

Estrangement from self and loss of meaningful personal identity are part of a long list of dangerous consequences which follow from a bureautechnocratic environment. In a very real sense they are the end products of all the demands bureautechnocracy makes upon societal members. More specifically, however, they follow directly from what Fromm has identified as the process of quantification and abstraction,[47] a process which

[45] *Labor Looks at Labor: A Conversation,* quoted in Marcuse, *One-Dimensional Man,* p. 20.

[46] Erich Fromm, *The Sane Society* (New York: Holt, Rinehart and Winston, 1955), p. 110.

[47] Ibid., p. 111.

is fundamental in and essential to a social system propelled by technological drivenness.

Bureautechnocracy depends upon quantification and abstraction in terms of processes, people, institutions, and things. For example, all economic activities have to be strictly quantifiable, measured with abstract symbols, and expressed in abstractions. "The exact comparison of economic processes quantified in figures, tell the manager whether and to what degree he is engaged in a profitable, that is to say, a meaningful business activity."[48] But the processes go much beyond this.

> This transformation of the concrete into the abstract has developed far beyond the balance sheet and the quantification of economic occurrences in the sphere of production. The modern businessman not only deals with millions of dollars, but also with millions of customers, thousands of stockholders, and thousands of workers and employees; all these people become so many pieces in a gigantic machine which must be controlled, whose effects must be calculated; each man eventually can be expressed as an abstract entity, as a figure, and on this basis economic occurrences are calculated, trends are predicted, decisions are made.[49]

Undoubtedly, without quantification and abstractification bureautechnocracy would be lacking in technological drivenness and would, most likely, collapse. "But in a society in which economic activities have become the main preoccupation of man, this process of quantification and abstractification has transcended the realm of economic production, and spread to the attitude of man to things, to people, and to himself."[50] We "abstractify" man. He is not a *person*, but a manager, a worker, or a buyer whose needs can be manipulated and whose capacity for work and involvement therein is expressed in functional terms.

[48] Ibid.
[49] Ibid., pp. 111–12.
[50] Ibid.

It is not surprising, therefore, that people are also *experienced* as abstractions, as things.

> To speak of a man as being "worth one million dollars," is to speak of him not any more as a concrete human person, but as an abstraction, whose essence can be expressed in a figure. It is an expression of the same attitude when a newspaper headlines an obituary with the words "Shoe Manufacturer Dies." Actually a *man* has died, a man with certain human qualities, with hopes and frustration, with a wife and children. It is true that he manufactured shoes, or rather, that he owned and managed a factory in which workers served machines manufacturing shoes; but if it is said that a "Shoe Manufacturer Dies," the richness and concreteness of a human life is expressed in the abstract formula of economic function.[51]

Any culture promotes that social character type in an individual which will permit the individual to survive in that culture. Some tribes among our Western Plains Indians, for example, produced a culture wherein aggressiveness and refusal to give in to pain were important human traits. Accordingly, infants who cried quickly learned to stop crying after having water poured into their nostrils. Bureautechnocracy in its turn has created a culture which makes its own demands—efficiency, consumption, impersonal relationships, and homogeneity. Accordingly, the individual, in order to survive, must renounce his individuality. Modern man has become a stranger to himself. "He does not experience himself as the center of his world. . . . [he is] out of touch with himself as he is out of touch with any other person. . . . He, like the others, is experienced as things are experienced."[52] Man has lost his sense of identity as man.

[51] Ibid., p. 116.
[52] Ibid., p. 120. As Jourard has stated, "Alienation from one's real self not only arrests one's growth as a person; it also tends to make a farce out of one's relationship with people" (*The Transparent Self* [Princeton: Van Nostrand, 1964], p. 25).

In the next chapter we will look at the problems of self-esteem and human degradation, along with bureautechnocracy's cultivated resistance to qualitative change.

CHAPTER 3

The Bitter Harvest

LOST SELF-ESTEEM

"I am a human being. Please do not fold, spindle, or mutilate." This plaintive entreaty, appearing on a sign borne by a youthful protestor in one of the "demonstrations" at the University of California (Berkeley) in 1965, eloquently expresses the primordial sense of defeat, lost self-esteem, and degradation which gnaws at modern man's psyche.

In this chapter we examine the nature, sources, and consequences of contemporary man's sense of "being done in" and the anxiety which leads from it. In addition, we examine a feature which inheres in bureautechnocracy and which suggests that forces leading to man's loss of self-esteem, etc., will not quickly disappear; namely, the system's cultivated resistance to qualitative change.

There exist in our bureautechnocratic culture several inherent characteristics or forces which generate and sustain conditions which lead to, and account for man's increasing sense of, degradation and lost self-esteem. Among these are the following:

(1) the instrumental conception of man inherent in bureautechnocracy, and the functional–commodity-exchange

patterns of personal and interpersonal evaluations which
follow;
(2) cultural cues which suggest to man that he is functionally expendable and thereby in danger of becoming personally as well as functionally obsolescent;
(3) bureautechnocratic demands that require men to engage
in (work at) activities and jobs which they have little
interest in doing and which are nonrewarding in terms
of the human qualities persons bring into these activities;
(4) bureautechnocratic pressures for seeking and finding
personal identity in the symbolic value attached to our
possessions;
(5) bureautechnocracy's need to produce vast quantities of
waste in the face of human need and misery.

These characteristics or forces inhere in a sociocultural environment of man's making. Fromm puts it this way:

> Man has created a world of man-made things as it never existed
> before. He has constructed a complicated social machine to
> administer the technical machine he built. Yet this whole
> creation of his stands over and above him. He does not feel
> himself as a creator and center, but as a servant of a Golem,
> which his hands have built. The more powerful and gigantic
> the forces are which he unleashes, the more powerless he feels
> himself as a human being. He confronts himself with his own
> forces embodied in things he has created, alienated from
> himself. He is owned by his own creation, and has lost owner-
> ship of himself.[1]

The first characteristic we cited above as bearing upon man's
sense of lost self-esteem is the instrumental conception of man inherent in bureautechnocracy. By "instrumental conception" we
mean that man is conceived of as a definable, quantifiable object,

[1] Erich Fromm, *The Sane Society* (New York: Holt, Rinehart and Winston, 1955), p. 125.

useful toward the attainment of some predefined system (bureautechnocratic) goal. Man is not in this conception seen as an
end unto himself, but only as an instrument possessing no basic
or enduring qualities. The instrumental (or tool) conception reveals itself in the arena of false need creation and manipulation,
and the reordering of Super Ego. In these instances—as in the instrumental conception itself—it is not man as man that is important, and whose needs are primary, but it is the system and
its needs which prevail. In short, bureautechnocracy generates
and sustains a cultural milieu wherein "subjects as well as objects
constitute instrumentalities in a whole that has its *raison d'etre*
in the accomplishments of its overpowering productivity."[2]

Bureautechnocracy's overpowering productivity (or, to use
Henry's phrase again, "technological drivenness") has created a
culture in which man sees himself and others as instruments.
Fromm speaks of this in terms of a "marketing orientation." The
marketing orientation refers to a concept of value wherein personal worth is equated with one's exchange or marketing value
as opposed to one's human qualities. The mature, productive,
self-assured, "free" person derives his sense of identity and
worth from within himself; he experiences himself "as the active
bearer of his own powers and richness . . . [not] as an impoverished 'thing,' dependent on powers outside of himself, unto
whom he has projected his living substance."[3] He does not evaluate his value or worth by solely or essentially ranking the
marketability of certain talents or skills which are his. He looks
beyond these to his "inner" self, to those qualities of which his
talents or skills are merely functions, or which determine the
purpose to which the skills are put and which determine the
relative emphasis he places upon those skills in arriving at his
identity. In the marketing orientation/instrumental conception,
however, man is conditioned not to look beyond the marketable

[2] Herbert Marcuse, *One-Dimensional Man* (Boston: Beacon Press, 1965),
p. 23.
[3] Fromm, *The Sane Society*, p. 125.

skills. He is pressured to depend upon powers outside of himself in the sense that the marketable skills in his possession are defined as marketable by outside criteria, and society judges his relative worth on the basis of these skills. Man in contemporary society, therefore, experiences his powers as commodities estranged from him. As Erich Fromm has stated:

> He is not one with them but they are masked from him because what matters is not his self-realization in the process of using them but his success in the process of selling them. Both his powers and what they create become estranged, something different from himself, something for others to judge and to use; thus his feeling of identity becomes as shaky as his self-esteem; it is constituted by the sum total of roles one can play; 'I am as you desire me' . . . .[4]

In a culture dominated by a marketing orientation, says Fromm, man's value or worth, as perceived by the individual, is dependent upon factors outside the individual, factors which reside in the needs of the system. Accordingly, man is defined as "good" in terms of system needs, and "goodness" is a function of the powers or skills possessed by the individual which are crucial to the system. In this sense, man's powers become commodities which can be exchanged for definitions of goodness and/or system rewards; they can be exchanged on a market which deals in human traffic, just as objects (cars, pencils, shoes, etc.) can be exchanged.[5]

[4] Erich Fromm, *Man for Himself*, in H. C. Bredemeier and Jackson Toby, eds., *Social Problems in America* (New York: John Wiley and Sons, 1960), p. 141.

[5] This discussion takes us back to something we discussed in Ch. 2, regarding man's functional placement in a bureautechnocratized world of work. A man's specialty—his function—fills a position, and it alone is important to that position, not the person as such. Accordingly, it is not Mr. Jones and his human qualities per se filling the position of executive vice-president for the Acme Corporation, but Jones the successful administrator and manager whose value and success in his position are defined in terms of skills (commodities) important to Acme.

Therefore, through "technological drivenness" bureautechnocracy creates a marketing orientation wherein individuals encounter and experience "self" and "other" as commodities, as
things which are saleable and "good" in terms of powers or
traits defined by system needs and exchangeable only in light of
system needs. One consequence of this "humans-as-commodi-
ties" principle is that "the difference between people is reduced
to a merely quantitative difference of being more or less successful, attractive, [saleable] hence valuable.[6] Like cars which can
be reduced to their price or exchange value, which can be quantified and described in proportionate terms (so many sedans
equal so many convertibles), human beings in bureautechnocracy can be reduced to their exchange value and quantified in
the light of their relative worth to one another.

> Their individuality, that which is peculiar and unique to them,
> is valueless and in a fact, a ballast. The meaning which the
> word "peculiar" has assumed is quite expressive of this atti-
> tude. Instead of denoting the greatest achievement of man—
> that of having developed his individuality—it has become al-
> most synonymous with "queer." The word, "equality," has also
> changed its meaning. The idea that all men are created equal
> implied that all men have the same fundamental right to be
> considered as ends in themselves and not as means. Today,
> "equality" has become equivalent to "interchangeability," and
> is the very negation of individuality. Equality, instead of being
> the condition for the development of each man's peculiarity,
> means the extinction of individuality, the "selflessness" char-
> acteristic of the marketing orientation. Equality was con-
> junctive with difference, but it has become synonymous with
> "indifference" and, indeed, indifference is what characterizes
> modern man's relationship to himself and to others.[7]

The instrumental conception of man, inherent in bureautechnocracy, is one of the major factors contributing to man's increas-

[6] Fromm, *Man for Himself*, p. 141.
[7] Ibid., pp. 141–42.

ing sense of degradation and decreasing self-esteem. Loss of self-esteem is a result of submission to normative (outside) criteria which circumscribe and define human and personal worth. Fromm again:

> Since modern man experiences himself both as the seller and as the commodity to be sold on the market, his self-esteem depends on conditions beyond his control. If he is "successful," he is valuable; if he is not, he is worthless. The degree of insecurity which results from this orientation can hardly be overestimated. If one feels that one's own value is not constituted primarily by the human qualities one possesses, but by one's success on a competitive market with ever-changing conditions, one's self-esteem is bound to be shaky and in constant need of confirmation by others. Hence one is driven to strive relentlessly for success, and any setback is a severe threat to one's self-esteem; helplessness, insecurity, and inferiority feelings are the result. If the vicissitudes of the market are judges of one's value, the sense of dignity and pride is destroyed.[8]

When human worth is determined in terms of success in an "open market," persons must compete with one another. And competition,[9] of course, is crucial to bureautechnocracy. In competition, however, someone wins—always at the expense of another. Karen Horney tells us about the consequences of this phenomenon:

> The psychic result of this situation is a diffuse hostile tension between individuals. Everyone is the real or potential competitor of everyone else. . . . The potential hostile tension between individuals results in a constant generation of fear—

---

[8] Ibid., p. 140.

[9] It should be recognized that even though competitiveness and the potential hostility that accompanies it pervades most human relationships, competition is not biologically conditioned. It is a function of certain cultural conditions which are very active in our culture and which are imposed upon societal members from cradle to grave.

fear of the potential hostility of others, reinforced by a fear of retaliation for hostilities of one's own. Another important source of fear in the normal individual is the prospect of failure. The fear of failure is a realistic one because, in general, the chances of failing are much greater than those of succeeding, and because failures in a competitive society entail a realistic frustration of needs. They mean not only economic insecurity, but also loss of prestige and all kinds of emotional frustrations.[10]

Overpowering productivity, "technological drivenness," competition, and the marketing orientation—all these interdependent and mutually supportive features of bureautechnocracy promote and sustain cultural conditions wherein "even the most normal person is constrained to feel that he amounts to something when successful, and is worthless if he is defeated. Needless to say, this presents a shaky basis for self-esteem."[11]

Inherent in the cultural milieu produced by bureautechnocracy are all sorts of cues which suggest to man that he is expendable and thereby in danger of becoming functionally obsolescent. In a society permeated by the marketing orientation, the possibility of functional obsolescence suggests, as a logical corollary, personal and human obsolescence. More specifically, if my worth or value, as determined by myself and others in light of the marketing orientation, is a function of my functional skills—my commodities—then the fleeting value of these commodities on the exchange market tells me that my own personal worth—and my identity—is transient and in danger of becoming obsolescent. Awareness of his functional placement in the system, and the fact that persons are viewed functionally in respect to their roles,

---

[10] Karen Horney, *The Neurotic Personality of Our Time* (New York: W. W. Norton, 1937), pp. 284–85.
[11] Ibid., p. 286.

brings home to man the fact that his place in the role depends upon certain functional capacities that can be instantly replaced. All this follows from an elementary need of bureautechnocracy: the security of this system depends upon and generates a constant pressure for *the institutionalization of relationships,* thus removing them from the uncertainties of individual "feelings" about, and human responses to them. Moreover, it is necessary for the relationships within the system to be determined in such a way that individuals will be interchangeable, thus freeing the system (a factory, corporation, school, i.e., any large bureautechnocratized social system) from dependence upon personal qualities. Functional placement in the system, emphasis upon commodity exchange value as opposed to human value, absence of human fealty or sentiment, interchangeability of individuals, and a system free of dependence upon personal qualities—all these contribute directly to man's increased sense of lost self-esteem. They "tell" man that "one's human capacities are in danger of becoming obsolete, and every man and woman therefore stands in peril of waking up one morning to discover that he is, too."[12]

Closely related to the problems associated with the functional or commodity exchange evaluation of human worth is the fact that bureautechnocracy requires many people to work at jobs in which they have little interest and in which there is little reward for individual contributions and little possibility for recognition.[13] This is a problem that will continue to grow as the acceleration rate of automation increases. A few years ago the problem of interesting and rewarding work had to do with assembly line and clerical workers. However, as machines continue to take over the productive process, more and more factory and clerical jobs are turned into routine, "machine-watching" tasks. The result shows itself in alienating conditions of work, con-

---

[12] Jules Henry, *Culture against Man* (New York: Random House, 1963), p. 23.
[13] See our earlier discussion of the power elite, pp. 24ff.

ditions which have "made many people spiritually useless to themselves."[14] Swados offers us some insight into this problem as it relates to the plight of factory workers.

> They know that there is a difference between working with your back and working with your behind. (I do not make the distinction between hand-work and brain-work, since we are all learning that white-collar work is becoming less and less brain-work.) They know that they work harder than the middle class for less money. Nor is it simply a question of status, that magic word so dear to the hearts of the sociologues, the new anatomizers of the American corpus. It is not simply status-hunger that makes a man hate work which pays *less* than other work he knows about, if *more* than any other work he has been trained for (the only reason my fellow-workers stayed on the assembly line, they told me again and again). It is not simply status-hunger that makes a man hate work that is mindless, endless, stupefying, sweaty, filthy, noisy, exhausting, insecure in its prospects, and practically without hope of advancement.

Swados goes on to tell us that a man hates factory work simply because it is degrading. His long and dreary hours are only going to buy him commodities, not human dignity. Swados then explains:

> Almost without exception, the men with whom I worked on the assembly line last year felt like trapped animals. Depending upon their age and personal circumstances, they were either resigned to their fate, furiously angry at *themselves* for what they were doing, or desperately hunting other work that would pay as well and in addition offer some variety, some prospect of change and betterment. They were sick of being pushed around by harried foremen (themselves more pitied than hated), sick of working like blinkered donkeys, sick of being

14 Henry, *Culture against Man,* p. 25.

dependent for their livelihood on a maniacal production-merchandising setup. . . .[15]

The alienating conditions of the world of work, though of greater intensity at the factory level, are not limited to this area. They are also increasingly a part of the white-collar world of work.

> The alienation of the white-collar man (like that of the la-borer) from both his tools and whatever he produces, the slavery that chains the exurbanite to the commuting timetable (as the worker is still chained to the time-clock), the anxiety that sends the white-collar man home with his briefcase for an evening's work (as it degrades the workingman into pleading for long hours of overtime), the displacement of the white-collar slum from the wrong side of the tracks to the suburbs (just as the working-class slum is moved from old-law tene-ments to skyscraper barracks)—all these mean to me that the white-collar man is entering (though his arms may be loaded with commodities) the grey world of the working man.[16]

Jules Henry has discussed this problem so well that we can put it in no better perspective than by quoting from him at length:

> Most people do the job they have to do regardless of what they want to do; technological drivenness has inexorable re-quirements, and the average man or woman either meets them or does not work. With a backward glance at the job-dreams of his pre-"labor force" days the young worker enters the oc-cupational system not where he would, but where he can; and his job-dream, so often an expression of his dearest self, is pushed down with all his other unmet needs to churn among them for the rest of his life. The worker's giving up an essential

---

[15] Harvey Swados, "The Myth of the Happy Worker," in Maurice Stein et al., eds., *Identity and Anxiety* (Glencoe, Ill.: The Free Press, 1960), p. 202.
[16] Ibid., p. 203.

part of himself to take a job, to survive and to enjoy himself as he may is the new renunciation, the new austerity; it is the technological weed that grows where the Vedic flower bloomed. What makes the renunciation particularly poignant is that it comes after an education that emphasizes exploitation of all the resources of the individual, and which has declared that the promise of democracy is freedom of choice.

This renunciation of the needs of the self—this latter-day self-lessness—is, paradoxically, a product of the most successful effort in human history to meet on a mass basis an infinite variety of material needs. The man who accepts such a renunciation does indeed approach fulfillment of the wants the engines of desire-production have stirred within him, and whoever refuses to renounce his very self will get few of the material things for which he has been taught to hunger.[17]

The importance of material goods in an environment which is dependent upon the acquisitiveness of people points to another cause of man's sense of lost self-esteem: bureautechnocratic pressures for seeking and finding personal identity in the symbolic value attached to our possessions. In today's society we increasingly judge ourselves as successful, hence of value, through automobiles, homes, fashions, i.e., through material goods. These things have always "told" us something about ourselves and others, but in bureautechnocracy they are conspicuously important. The car, the stereo set, the Florida tan, etc., are for conspicuous use; they confer status on the owner and symbolize aspects of his identity and worth.

The fact that we increasingly seek and find personal identity, and evaluate others, through possessions, suggests how important bureautechnocracy is in shaping our identities. It is the system which has produced the all-important possessions and which created and manipulated our "need" for them. Toby and Bredemeier put it best when they wrote:

[17] Henry, *Culture against Man*, p. 25.

> We may make a religion out of self-gratification (hedonism).
> . . . We . . . also make a religion of *things*, of the tangible
> entities which seem more real to a population impressed with
> the triumphs of atomic physics and antibiotics. The worship
> of things (materialism) is not, however, undertaken with a
> clear conscience. Americans are far more interested in sym-
> bolic rather than the physical aspect of cars and houses and
> clothes. Americans are materialistic by default—because they
> try to use "things" to express their search for the meaning of
> existence.[18]

There are two very important but disturbing aspects of this
"religion," this search for identity in material goods.

First, the identity that a person may find through the symbolic
value of his possessions is circumscribed by built-in, planned
obsolescence. The sense of pride, ownership, and status one may
find in his shiny new convertible, for example, is limited by one's
knowledge that the new car is only "good" (mechanically and
stylistically) for a planned and limited period of time. Because
of this limitation, we find it necessary to keep on buying, to get
a new car, etc., every year in order to make more enduring those
transient, fleeting, and nonintegrative values which our possessions symbolize. Furthermore, our awareness of the planned
obsolescence, and the fact that a "newer" model will revitalize
the dying value of our symbolic possession, makes us more dependent upon the system—and its representatives—which generates the obsolence-revitalization-obsolescence, ad infinitum.
"Originally, the idea of consuming more and better things was
meant to give man a happier, more satisfied life. Consumption
was a means to an end, that of happiness. It now has become an
aim itself. The constant increase of needs forces us to an ever-
increasing effort, it makes us dependent on these needs and on
the people and institutions by whose help we attain them."[19]

The "religion" also confounds the putting together of a value

[18] Bredemeier and Toby, *Social Problems in America*, p. 77.
[19] Fromm, *The Sane Society*, pp. 134–35.

system. Personal identity which carries meaning and self-esteem is rooted in any number of things, but basic to such identity is attachment to a pattern of values which is integrated (one value suggests and is interdependent with another), fairly stable through time (not susceptible to day-to-day change), and which allows the individual to be himself—to exhibit characteristic (not necessarily predictable) behavior. In short, such a pattern of values permits the individual to be a consistent human being whose actions can be identified as characteristically his own; he experiences *himself* as the maker and bearer of his own strength and worth. He does not have to measure his worth in terms of criteria external to and created by something or someone other than himself.

The material goods with which we surround ourselves do not fit together into a meaningful, integrative whole. They do not result in an identity consciousness which carries emotional-intellectual security and esteem. Our goods do not imply stable or continuous values. They are not founded upon, nor do they imply, "those values which are at the top of the hierarchy—the beliefs, faiths and ideals which integrate and determine subordinate values."[20] Our possessions imply the opposite of the integrative values; they suggest materialism, impulse release, profit, discontinuity, competition, aggressiveness, superficiality, and so on. In bureautechnocracy, therefore, a person motivated by the drives of competition and acquisitiveness will discover a cultural milieu compatible with his personality. On the other hand, a person motivated by more integrative and humane values is at a disadvantage; these values are much more difficult to find and sustain once found. Furthermore, our society offers little reward to those who elect to seek them out. Values of this sort, therefore, lack compelling power, and it is no wonder that modern man turns to those which are compelling: the false need values of bureautechnocracy.

[20] Allen Wheelis, *The Quest for Identity* (New York: W. W. Norton, 1958), p. 200.

The fact that man's identity is increasingly anchored in his possessions has made him a "great" consumer. He consumes baseball games, "moving pictures, newspapers and magazines, books, lectures, natural scenery, social gatherings, in the same alienated and abstractified way in which he consumes the commodities he has bought. He does not participate actively, he wants to 'take in' all there is to be had, and to have as much as possible."[21]

The alienated consumer, the alienated worker, the self-renouncing fearful competitor, the prospective obsolescent functionary, the unesteemed person feels psychologically isolated. As Karen Horney has noted, "even when he has many contacts with others, even when he is happily married, he is emotionally isolated."[22] It is this emotional isolation, so difficult to endure, which intensifies modern man's need for affection and belongingness; and it is this intensified need which accounts, in part, for our easy susceptibility to homogenizing forces. Attachment to "the crowd," our "other-directedness"—these are attempts to satisfy our great need for affection in an age which disavows affection and intimacy.

Up to this point we have discussed four major causes of man's sense of lost self-esteem and degradation: (1) the instrumental conception of man inherent in bureautechnocracy, and the commodity-exchange patterns of personal and interpersonal evaluation which follow; (2) man's awareness of his expendability on the market of human exchange, and his consequent fear regarding his possible functional (hence personal) obsolescence; (3) the nonrewarding, alienating conditions inherent in the world of work; and (4) bureautechnocratic pressures for seeking and locating personal identity in the nonintegrative, nonenduring symbolic values found in our material goods. There remains

[21] Fromm, *The Sane Society*, p. 136.
[22] Horney, *The Neurotic Personality of Our Time*, p. 286.

one more bureautechnocratic phenomenon which deserves special comment: the production of vast quantities of waste in the face of great human need and misery.

In order for bureautechnocracy to maintain its present rate of economic and social expansion, it is necessary to produce, consume, and store great quantities of waste. We store huge quantities of excess produce, we pay farmers to keep land out of production, we seek to control inflation by creating greater unemployment, in order to meet the self-protective imperatives of bureautechnocracy. All this we do in spite of our knowledge that there are millions of human beings who are literally starving to death and millions of others who just get by to live a life shortened by physiological and psychological misery. In the United States alone, the problem of poverty and near poverty is immense.[23] Myrdal summarized the problem in this fashion:

If poverty be defined as having to live on an annual income of under $4,000 for multiple-person families and $2,000 for unattached individuals, 38 million Americans, or more than onefifth of the nation, were poor in 1960. In deprivation (defined as above poverty but short of the requirements for what in America is now considered a modestly comfortable standard of living—from $4,000 to $6,000 for families and from $2,000 to $3,000 for unattached individuals) were more than 39 mil-

[23] Homogenizing forces are interesting to examine in their relation to impoverished or near-impoverished groups in our society. These "other Americans" have been cut off from the material advantages most of us enjoy. Our efforts to alleviate these conditions have been minimal but, where exercised, they are focused upon integrating and assimilating the excluded into the mainstream; in the process, other values have been lost sight of. Accordingly, the base of bureautechnocracy is "broadened as it assimilates its wearied challengers. It might almost be a trick, the way such politics work. It is rather like the ruse of inveighing someone you wish to capture to lean all his weight on a door you hold closed . . . and then, all of a sudden, throwing it open. He not only winds up inside, where you want him, but he comes crashing in full tilt" (Theodore Roszak, *The Making of a Counter Culture* [Garden City, N.Y.: Doubleday, 1969], p. 14).

lion people, or again more than one-fifth of the nation. Utter destitution—the situation of people with less than half the poverty income—was the destiny of more than 12½ million Americans, or nearly 7 percent of the population of the United States.[24]

These figures for our country alone suggest a great deal about the human misery that exists on this planet. Man—a man—cannot help but feel degraded; he does not count and he knows it. Those who are impoverished feel this degradation directly; the very rise in productivity which produces greater numbers of goods for the affluent prolongs the plight of the poor. As society becomes more technological and demands more skills, those who are afforded opportunities for education and training move up the scale and are allowed to participate in system rewards. The poor, at a disadvantage from the beginning, become more disadvantaged. The poor "are the victims of the very inventions that have provided a higher living standard for the rest of society. They are upside-down in the economy, and for them greater productivity often means worse jobs; agricultural advance becomes hunger."[25] One of the ironies of bureautechnocracy is that it possesses a technology that could permit all citizens to participate in enjoying satisfaction of not only basic needs, but even the false ones. Nevertheless, in a time of material plenty and great false-need satisfaction, millions of people go through a shortened life unable to satisfy the most elementary of human needs.

The production of waste in the face of human suffering says something about the place of man vis-à-vis bureautechnocracy. In order to adjust to this situation with the least amount of psychic pain, man represses that which he sees with his own eyes. He represses those pangs of self which tell him that, as part

[24] Gunnar Myrdal, *Challenge to Affluence* (New York: Random House, 1965), p. 50.

[25] Michael Harrington, *The Other America: Poverty in the United States* (Baltimore: Penguin Books, 1962), p. 19.

of the genus man, he does not stand high in the order of bureau-technocratic needs.[26] He submits to the demands of bureautech-nocracy. He learns to put in the place of his inner self a high and rising standard of living. In so doing, he must perpetuate that which degrades him "because technological drivenness can sur-vive as a cultural configuration . . . only if it becomes a moral law, a kind of conscience."[27] Technological drivenness is becom-ing a "kind of conscience" in the sense that (as we noted earlier) bureautechnocracy is successfully reordering the Super Ego.

The drive toward making bureautechnocracy and its needs, including technological drivenness, a way of life, a kind of con-science or moral imperative, gains momentum; as it does, the doors to other alternatives are being closed, and the resistance to qualitative change is becoming greater.

RESISTANCE TO QUALITATIVE CHANGE

A curiosity of contemporary life is the role of change. No one can gainsay the fact that we are in the midst of extensive and rapid change. Furthermore, as individuals we have come to in-ternalize, as a sort of moral imperative, the belief that adapt-ability to change is indicative of good mental health. This is re-flected in the social behavior type held out as desirable for our times: namely, that person who possesses the ability to contin-ually modify himself, to change his attitudes and/or behavior patterns to everchanging conditions. In short, bureautechnoc-racy promotes, through advertising and false need manipulation, that type of personality wherein the following features prevail: "The light touch supplants the firm grip; the launcher of trial balloons replaces the committed man. [It is a character type

---

[26] It is a well-known psychological fact that one cannot be repressive and at the same time have a subjectively well-defined conception of one's needs, aspirations, and self.

[27] Henry, *Culture against Man*, p. 25.

which] . . . avoids final decisions, keeps everything subject to revision, and stands ready to change course when the winds change. The key words of our time are flexibility, adjustment, and warmth—as, for our grandfathers, they were work, thrift, and will."[28]

The flexibility and adaptability to change[29] required by bureautechnocracy are perhaps argued for too well. In one sense, not much really changes in our society. As Galbraith has pointed out, "The economic system of the United States is praised on all occasions of public ceremony as a largely perfect structure. This is so elsewhere also. It is not easy to perfect what has been perfected. There is massive change but, except as the output of goods increases, all remains as before."[30] Galbraith may be overstating the case when he says that "*all* remains as before"; many changes do take place, and with significant impact. He is correct, however, in the sense that what is crucial to bureautechnocracy does remain the same as before in the face of great and numerous changes.

There are three major types of change which take place in social systems. They may affect each other but they can—and in our society usually do—occur relatively independently of one another. These three types of changes are (1) changes in the material aspects of the culture, to include material products (clothes, food, appliances, etc.) and institutions; (2) changes in the means or operational methods for attaining the goals of

---

28 Wheelis, *The Quest for Identity*, p. 85.

29 For purposes of clarity it may be helpful to review some terminology. Anthropologists often use the term *cultural change* in their studies. This is a broad term, usually applicable to alterations in a culture's patterns—changes in technology, art, food, clothing, customs, and social relationships. Sociologists use the term *social change* to designate primarily changes in the nonmaterial culture—that is, changes in values, mores, institutions, and social behavior. Our analysis in this chapter will suggest that we have had and are more susceptible to *cultural* change, i.e., for the most part *material* change.

30 John Kenneth Galbraith, *The New Industrial State* (New York: New American Library, 1967), p. 13.

the system; and (3) changes in the goals themselves. While changes in the material aspects of the culture are commonplace, changes in means and goals are both difficult to attain; changes in the means, nevertheless, are more common than changes in goals. Change in our world of values, attitudes, and beliefs about societal goals is essentially conservative. This is easily explained. The greatest resistance to change in any social system issues from and concerns matters which are connected with what is held to be sacred. In our society, the goals and values of bureautechnocracy—profit, achievement, expansiveness, acquisitiveness, technological drivenness—are so embedded in our way of life, and hence our psyches, that they have become sacrosanct. As our society becomes increasingly homogenized and interdependent, these goals become increasingly impervious to change by locking themselves to each other.

> It seems that the leaders of business, labor, and government . . . have today many more similarities in their viewpoints than differences. The present leaders naturally attempt to use the past to present the image of the future, conserving the values and attitudes which have made present institutions and organizations successful. They search for ways in which the present technological changes can be viewed as normal evolution. The problem, as seen through the eyes of our leaders, is to find agencies for our present imbalances, to provide stimulus to the already existent institutions, and to take care to provide the balance between change and stability in such a way that our basic economic and political systems suffer minimum change. Their approach in general is to seek out adjustments, to intensify or weaken various operative forces, and to make present institutional formats work with minimum change. This is the conservative view and it guarantees that the future will preserve to the maximum extent the shape of those ideas which guaranteed success in the past.[31]

[31] Charles R. DeCarlo, "Perspectives in Technology," quoted in Donald N. Michael, *The Unprepared Society* (New York: Basic Books, 1968), p. 94.

Societal and cultural interlocking, intensified and legitimized by bureautechnocracy's leaders and representatives, gives rise to a sociocultural condition wherein the norms of the culture operate, vis-à-vis change, as do habits in the individual. Habits might not unreasonably be called "neurologically based resistance to relearning, once one has learned successful behavior."[32] Psychologically (at the individual level), habits "protect" the individual from exposing himself to changes which may put in jeopardy a satisfying self-image. This is also the case at the societal level. The norms of bureautechnocracy, intensified by the homogenizing and interdependency forces therein, serve to protect the system and its goals from change. Watson put it this way: "Norms in social systems correspond to habits in individuals. They are customary and expected ways of behaving. . . . Because norms are shared by many participants, they cannot easily change. Above all, the usual individual cannot change them. He can get himself rejected for deviate behavior, but the norms will persist."[33]

The norms of bureautechnocracy are such that we have come to accept change in material aspects of the culture and, to some extent, in the means or technology to bureautechnocracy's goals. It is in this sense that the social character type we discussed earlier is being molded to accept change. On the other hand, we have been indoctrinated to believe that changes in bureautechnocracy's goals are unwarranted. In this regard the system's ability to contain change relative to goals is easily explained by a relatively elementary principle of social change: attitudes which have been instilled in us as norms, attitudes with which we have become, through indoctrination, ego-involved, are among the most difficult to change since they seemingly provide us with "security" and "satisfaction." Conversely, atti-

[32] Michael, *The Unprepared Society*, p. 93.
[33] Goodwin Watson, "Resistance to Change," in W. G. Bennis, K. D. Benne, and R. Chin, eds., *The Planning of Change*, 2nd ed. (New York: Holt, Rinehart and Winston, 1968), p. 493.

tudes are most flexible when there has been little or no indoctrination, or when they are structured by social norms in such a way as to make them susceptible to changing tides. We have been acculturated into expecting changes in the material aspects of our culture to be "good" and "necessary" changes. Our attitudes about style, fashion, and function, for example, are such that we hold to them lightly, ready to change them as society introduces new materials to replace the old. The firmness with which we hold to bureautechnocracy's goals on the one hand, and the flexibility we have in regard to material and fleeting values on the other, are attested to by the fact that in bureautechnocracy we automatically identify change in the latter with progress. Change and progress, however, are not synonymous. Progress is change in a particular direction. Philosophically, therefore, one might offer any number of definitions depending upon *directions* which are perceived as "good" or, at the very least, beneficial. Some cultural theorists say, for example, that change is progress when change is in the direction of reducing magic and superstition, and increases rational methods of solving problems. Others might say that change is progress when there is growth in science. Still others might argue that significant social and/or cultural change, hence progress, occurs only when human misery is reduced. In any case, we will use our own value judgments here and say that change is progress when it is in the direction of opening up choices in goals, and toward opening up choices made with discrimination. We are suggesting, therefore, that change writ large is progress when it is in the direction of enhancing man's freedom, man's ability to choose new goals discriminately. Ask yourself, however, if change which leads to the following—discussed throughout this book as consequences of bureautechnocratic demands—can be defended as progress:

Homogeneity
Mimesis

Technological drivenness
Alienation
Repression
Fear
Hostility
Isolation
Anxiety
Noninvolvement
Loss of self-esteem
Loss of personal responsibility
Dehumanization
Identity crisis
Renunciation of self

One would be hard put to defend as progress change which leads in the direction of the above. Yet this is what has happened in bureautechnocracy. The system's legitimizers—corporations, government, advertising, labor, etc.—promote and sustain an environment where the above phenomena are occuring at an increasing rate; they still identify as progress changes which generate these phenomena. Bureautechnocracy has been quite successful in convincing us that the type of changes we see about us are synonymous with progress. We Americans have come to abhor stability. We have been indoctrinated into believing that it is the opposite of progress. Yet technological drivenness, the motivating determinant for constant expansion, has become an end in itself and, in a perverted way, has come to insure stability. "It is a rare advertisement that emphasizes permanence or stability as such, since in . . . [bureautechnocracy] expansion *is* stability. That is to say, cultural maximizers in America abhor stability; what interests them, or better, what drives them, is expansion, and the permanence of their world is seen in terms of its limitless growth."[34]

Cultural and social anthropologists teach us that societies which are largely homogenized and characterized by dominat-

[34] Henry, *Culture against Man,* p. 33.

ing, interdependent, mutually supportive patterns of organization, control, goals, and behavior are the societies most resistant
to change in regard to the nonmaterial (values, goals, ideals,
etc.) aspects of culture. For example, preliterate societies which
are permeated by dominating, mutually supportive patterns of
ceremony and ritual are loath to respond to change-stimulating
ideas which may impact upon the "ultimate" values or goals to
which the ceremony and ritual are related. Southern European
countries, dominated by the Roman Catholic church, the influence of which reaches into all of life's activities in this region,
have shown great resistance to change. The class system in
Great Britain, a dominant cultural configuration pattern around
which most social and/or cultural activities have centered, has
contributed to the containment of change in that country. Ger-
many's Prussian cultural pattern—again impacting upon many
of that society's major life activities—functioned to contain
change in the value or goal culture of that country. We could
cite numerous other examples, but what should be recognized is
this: pluralistic societies are lacking in dominating, mutually
supportive patterns of organization, control, goals, and values.
Such societies, the anthropologists tell us, are also the most susceptible to change in regard to the nonmaterial aspects of their
culture. One can inferentially argue, therefore, in the following
manner:

Bureautechnocracy is the dominant cultural configuration
pattern of our time.

This dominant pattern manifests itself in mutually supportive,
interpendent patterns of organization, control, values, and
behavior.

Societies characterized by dominant cultural configuration
patterns are very resistant to change in the nonmaterial aspects
of culture.

Therefore, bureautechnocracy is resistant to, and capable of
containing, change in the nonmaterial aspects of culture.

It is for these reasons that observers of the contemporary scene comment to the effect that in the midst of seemingly great change "all remains as before." There is danger in this when "all remains as before" implies that the imperatives of bureautechnocracy, and hence their consequences, remain with us. This danger is augmented by the fact that in bureautechnocracy we do not rely or depend upon overt authority, but rather on subtle and anonymous authority as it is represented in the underlying intellectual framework or ideology of the system. We shall examine this in the next two chapters.

CHAPTER 4

The Supporting Ideology

"Give me a dozen healthy infants, well-formed, and my own specified world to bring them up in and I'll guarantee to take any one at random and train him to become any type of specialist. I might select doctor, lawyer, artist, merchant-chief and yes, even beggar-man and thief, regardless of his talents, penchants, tendencies, ability, vocations, and race of his ancestors."

—J. B. Watson, *Behaviorism*

SCIENTIFIC LIBERALISM

Watson was convinced that behavior was simply the result of conditioned reflexes, and that if society would make up its mind as to what it wanted in terms of character types, psychologists with data and proper equipment could turn out any human type deemed desirable. Watson's confidence seems to have been well grounded, and several features of our contemporary society would confirm it were he still with us. But his position is benign in comparison to the following narrative which could be a description of a not-too-distant future "nursery":

The hands of all the four thousand electric clocks in all the Bloomsbury Centre's four thousand rooms marked twenty-seven minutes past two. "This hive of industry," as the Director was fond of calling it, was in the full buzz of work. Everyone was busy, everything in ordered motion. Under the microscopes, their long tails furiously lashing, spermatozoa were burrowing head first into eggs; and, fertilized, the eggs were expanding, dividing, or if bokanovskified, budding and breaking up into whole populations of separate embryos. From the Social Predestination Room the escalators went rumbling down into the basement, and there, in the crimson darkness, stewingly warm on their cushion of peritoneum and gorged with blood-surrogate and hormones, the foetuses grew and grew or, poisoned, languished into a stunted Epsilonhood. With a faint hum and rattle, the moving racks crawled imperceptibly through the weeks and the recapitulated aeons to where, in the Decanting Room, the newly-unbottled babes uttered their first yell of horror and amazement.[1]

Is Huxley, perhaps even Watson, stretching things too far? Or are we, when we say that the above "could be a description of a not-too-distant future nursery"? Perhaps, in the sense that what is asserted and described here is outside the realm of present, direct experience. But they (and we) are not going too far in the sense that these assertions and descriptions are the logical consequences which follow from particular choices among views of human nature and the control of it. Behavioral and social scientists take it for granted that their findings will be used in the prediction and control of human behavior. Their beliefs in this regard, and the fact that their findings follow from a particular methodology with its own assumptions about human nature, do not make Watson or Huxley too "far out." And their findings, along with the use to which they are put, are indicative of the fact that their beliefs (about the practical utility of their findings) are well grounded.

[1] Aldous Huxley, *Brave New World* (New York: Harper Bantam Edition, 1958), p. 98.

To illustrate this real condition, and its potential, we have borrowed some material from Carl Rogers's *On Becoming a Person*. Rogers illustrates what we have learned from the behavioral and social sciences about controlling human behavior:

(1) We know how to predict, with considerable accuracy, which individuals will be successful college students, industrial executives, insurance salesmen, and the like.

(2) We know how to predict, with considerable accuracy, how radical or conservative a potential business executive will be.

(3) We know how to predict which members of an organization will be troublemakers for the organization.

(4) We can select those persons who are easily persuaded, who will conform to group pressures, or those who will not yield.

(5) We know how to establish conditions which will result in increased psychological rigidity in members of a group.

(6) We know how to establish conditions which will result in increased productivity, originality, and morale.

(7) We know a great deal about how to establish conditions which will influence consumer responses and/or public opinion.

(8) We know how to influence the buying behavior of individuals by setting up conditions which provide satisfaction for needs of which they are unconscious, but which we have been able to determine.

(9) We know how to establish conditions under which many individuals will report as true, judgments which are contrary to the evidence of their senses.

(10) We know how to change the opinions of an individual in a selected direction, without his even becoming aware of the stimuli which changed his opinion.

(11) We know how to influence psychological moods, and behavior, through drugs.

(12) We know how to provide psychological conditions which will provide vivid hallucinations and other abnormal reactions in otherwise normal individuals.

(13) We know the attitudes which, if provided by a counselor or a therapist, will be predictably followed by certain constructive personality and behavior changes in the client.

(14) We know how to disintegrate a man's personality structure, dissolving his self-confidence, destroying the concept he has of himself, and making him dependent on another.

(15) We know how to use a person's own words to open up whole troubled areas in his experience.[2]

More than anything else, these statements reflect the potential we possess for making Watson's world a reality. This potential has been partially realized through bureautechnocratic efforts at organization and control of human beings—for example, the deliberate creation and manipulation of false needs, the reordering of Super Ego, and the reality of consequences of mimesis. The possibility of a Watsonian world is found in an ideology which is increasingly dominating our way of life. Our ever increasing subservience to a sort of supraorganic bureautechnocracy did not simply come about—we have been guided to this condition by a system of belief, a rationale grounded in social action, which penetrates deeply into psychological and philosophical thought and which provides the ideological foundation of bureautechnocracy. For want of a better label, we call this ideological foundation *scientific liberalism*. We use the prefix "scientific" because we wish to separate the liberalism we will discuss from that which is usually associated with political and economic policies and programs. More important, however, we want to emphasize the place and role of science, particularly scientific method, in this system of thought.

[2] Carl Rogers, *On Becoming a Person* (Boston: Houghton Mifflin, 1961), pp. 366–75.

American intellectual liberalism has long expressed a general disdain for systems of social thought that involve the use of ideology for purposes of organizing and manipulating the values or motivating determinants of man's behavior. This disdain has been expressed against such diverse ideologies as fascism, nazism, Marxism, and political and philosophical reactionism. In very recent times this disdain has been expressed against the anti-liberal so-called New Left.

The anti-theology *stance* of liberals follows from, among other things, their belief that ideology connotes "systematically misleading misconception, unrealistic and hence ineffectual idealism and utopianism, [and] above all the notion that ideas themselves are, or can be, sources of human liberation."[3] American liberals, therefore, like to advertise that their "school of thought" is not to be regarded as "a rigid ideology nor a dogmatic system."[4] To link ideology with liberalism and/or science, as we are doing in this chapter, not surprisingly stirs indignation in American liberals. Science, we are told, is above systems of thought, transcends ideology, and is its foe. Furthermore, the spirit and even the tradition of modern liberalism is, we are told, the enemy of ideology. We believe, however, that what we call scientific liberalism is ideological in nature and consequences, and we hope to show this by first looking at the nature of ideology followed by an examination of scientific liberalism and its ideological character. Also, we will look briefly at some of the consequences of scientific liberalism.

The term *ideology* is vague and abrasive. Ideologies grow out of some political or social condition. More often than not such conditions are, or appear to be, the breeding grounds for various ills. The ideologue seizes upon such conditions and makes them

[3] Henry David Aiken, "Morality and Ideology," in Richard T. De George, ed., *Ethics and Society: Original Essays on Contemporary Moral Problems* (Garden City, N.Y.: Doubleday Anchor Books, 1966), p. 150.

[4] Arthur Schlesinger, Jr., quoted in Harry K. Girvetz, *The Evolution of Liberalism* (New York: Collier-Macmillan, 1963), p. 17.

the *cause celebre* for his point of view. It is in this regard that Hook tells us ideology refers to "the fundamental beliefs about nature, society, and man which any group offers in justification of the direction and good of its political activity."[5] Huntington means by ideology "a system of ideas concerned with the distribution of political and social values and acquiesced in by a significant social group."[6] From these two definitions we can infer that ideology refers to an aggregate of ideas, beliefs, and modes of thinking characteristic of particular groups interested in furthering their beliefs, usually in opposition to those which prevail. But ideology means more than this. As Aiken has noted:

> An ideology is to be understood in terms of its active function or role as a determinant of one's general comportment as the member of a social group. If by a "way of life," one means not just a series of individual choices or decisions, but a more or less authoritative and comprehensive frame by means of which the members of a social group, conceived as members, organize their major activities, then an ideology may be taken to represent, whether in part or in whole, a social way of life. It is, so to say, *the controlling conceptual frame for such a way of life.*[7]

Ideologies, then, are goal oriented—directive. They "articulate goals, ideals, standards of justification, rules of legitimation, validation, and verification."[8] Also, as implied in the above definitions, ideologies contain meta-beliefs; that is, they "provide supporting contexts of belief concerning the nature of the world, man's place in it, the nature and condition of man himself, his history and institutions, and, not least, the major categorical

---

[5] Sidney Hook, *Political Power and Personal Freedom* (New York: Collier, 1959), p. 141.

[6] S. P. Huntington, "Conservatism as an Ideology," *The American Political Science Review* 51 (June, 1957): 454.

[7] Aiken, "Morality and Ideology," p. 161. Italics ours.

[8] Ibid.

bases of interpretation through which various forms of thought and expression are, and are to be, construed and interrelated."[9]

From these definitions we can infer that an ideology has the following characteristics:

(1) It is a pattern of thought containing ideas about the nature of the world, society, man, and his place and prospects therein.

(2) It is goal-oriented and therefore directive.

(3) It operates as the controlling conceptual frame by way of which those who identify with it organize and live out their life activities.

(4) It specifies the major bases of interpretation through which all of the above are to be expressed. It defines the "good" and the "bad," and it prescribes the ways to determine same.

An ideology may satisfy certain psychological, social, and/or logical needs—usually it is held to with a great deal of fervor that often borders on fanaticism—but it does not necessarily represent "truth." And the fervor reflects itself in the ideologue's messianic behavior; he seeks to convert others to his point of view by preaching about the "saving" qualities of his beliefs. More than what we have offered here could be used to describe the nature of ideology, but the important point is that an ideology corresponds to a creed wherein beliefs about nature, man, and society are offered as "true" and "correct," and those who identify with the creed seek to win others over to it.

What we call scientific liberalism owes its character to both science and the outlooks of what we might distinguish as *modern* liberalism. To be more specific, the "liberal" thinking which goes into scientific liberalism is not, like classical liberalism, radically individualistic and hostile to governmental and/or bureaucratic

[9] Ibid., pp. 161–62.

regulation. On the contrary, modern liberalism, though attaching itself to individualism, is quite comfortable with government and bureaucratic regulation.

Among liberalism's fundamental guiding principles is the conviction that man betters his lot more efficiently by the material reconstruction of his environment than by changing his philosophy. More specifically, the modern liberal or scientific liberal is convinced that control of environment, be it the natural or social environment, is *the* most appropriate means to a happy and "good" life. This belief is reflected in the fact that modern/scientific liberals take an "engineering" approach to social action. For example, we use the medium of television to create a saleable image for a candidate for the presidency of the United States. We construct new cities from scratch, "building" into these cities social and cultural conditions intended to meet what are perceived as certain social-psychological needs of the prospective inhabitants. We build huge apartment complexes with "built-in" features intended to meet just about all physical and perceived social needs of those who will live in these complexes. Applying human skill to the mastery of nature and social systems is a principal preoccupation of the modern liberal, as it has been for our society. "Social engineering and applied social science, as exemplified in our advertising, our organization of factories, our military institutions, and our schools, have flourished here as nowhere else."[10] Though modern liberals would agree that social engineering does not necessarily issue in virtue, they would also agree, however, that *it is virtuous.*

A second fundamental principle of modern liberalism is a consistent secular approach to political and social affairs. As Frankel states:

> Except in countries where there has been a long tradition of clerical control, liberalism has not been antireligious or anti-

[10] Charles Frankel, *The Case for Modern Man* (Boston: Beacon Press, 1959), p. 38.

clerical as such. But it has usually stood for the doctrine of the separation of Church and State, and for antipathy to ecclesiastical control of key social activities like education or politics. From Locke and Voltaire on, liberals have argued that it is sufficient to consult human interests in this world when evaluating a social proposal or a political order. It has treated religious and philosophical beliefs as private affairs, of ultimate moment, perhaps, to the individual's salvation and to his sense of the meaning of life, but without political significance as such. In discussing the foundations of political authority it has confined itself to purely secular and naturalistic considerations—the minimizing of violence, the protection of property, the maximizing of pleasure—which might have equal cogency for men of any denomination, or of none.[11]

Frankel goes on to isolate the features of scientific liberalism which most concern us here:

> With the triumphs of modern science . . . [scientific] liberals have distinctively emphasized, men can finally hope with some realism to remake their society by objective and nonpartisan methods of inquiry. The notion that science can be the central organizing agency for modern society is thus a distinctive feature of [scientific] liberalism. Conversely, the story of . . . [scientific] liberalism is the story of a progressively more emphatic denial that scientific methods can be limited in what they study or in what they disturb. In its largest terms . . . [scientific] liberalism has been the outlook of men who have felt that, with the emergence of science, modern society has a fox in its bosom.[12]

An overriding faith in science and its methods is the hallmark of modern liberalism. Although it is composed of other major and essential features, some of them discussed here, science either

[11] Ibid., p. 29.
[12] Ibid., p. 34.

gave birth to these other features or permeates them. For example, the secular approach to political and social affairs is a function of the modern liberal's attachment to science which tells him that nonsecular and/or theological, metaphysical concerns are beyond the scope of science. The influence of science is also seen in the modern liberal's attachment to the reconstruction of man's social and natural environment; his "engineering" approach to this reconstruction is a function of, and pervaded by, scientific methodology. Whether it is economic policy, dealing with the problems of poverty, or organizing our schools, the modern liberal looks to the methods and findings of science to guide him in formulating and making decisions.

Essentially, it is the pervasive influence of science in modern liberalism which makes it possible for us to discuss *scientific* liberalism as a single and continuing activity, i.e., an ideology. Furthermore, it is this emphasis upon science, constituting in effect a new rationalism,[13] which makes scientific liberalism the major supportive element for bureautechnocracy. Let us take a look at this new rationalism and some of its consequences.

NEORATIONALISM

Neorationalism cannot be ascribed in toto to any particular philosopher or philosophy. Rationalism, as typically used in philosophy, refers to those generic schools of traditional philosophy which have as their core the argument that man has the power or potential to know because of his inherent ability to reason. As such, man was said to be in possession of certain powers which, when exercised, would enable him to lead a "good life"—that is, a life which is free from labor and ugliness.

[13] Since it is this emphasis upon a new rationalism which largely accounts for the ideological character of scientific liberalism, and for the support bureautechnocracy finds therein, we will frequently use the term neorationalism in the remaining portions of this chapter.

Man, for the rationalist, is par excellence the rational animal. It is rationality which distinguishes him from other creatures. ... The classical rationalists ... conceived the exercise of reason teleologically as man's own distinctive and proper end. But they also conceived it in quasi-administrative terms, as the faculty which properly coordinates and controls all other human faculties, activities, and affairs. It is, or ought to be, the master of the passions and emotions. If certain other ends are also inherent in human nature, reason not only discovers the means to their realization, but where they conflict, it is empowered and entitled to reorient and harmonize them in various appropriate ways.[14]

Neorationalism has a philosophical and historical link with the traditional point of view, but it is not to be identified with it. Neorationalism accepts the core of traditional rationalism as described above and, as we shall see, shares some of its elitism (i.e., truth available to those who have the time to develop the means to truth), but the principles of the new rationalism are to be found in the norms of scientific logic and exact science. Theories of knowledge which fall under the general rubric of empiricism and/or positivism are virtually the paradigms of neorationalism. The new rationalism, therefore, is not merely a *theory* of reason and rationality as in the traditional view but, given its empirical and positivistic essence, it is also a "perspective upon human experience and conduct which ascribes to reason and rationality [uniquely conceived] a central and controlling place in our scheme of things."[15]

Scientific knowledge is at once the aim and intellectual apologia of the new rationality and scientific liberalism. The principles of knowledge and knowing are, therefore, explicit:

Knowledge is ... viewed largely in verification terms, and one who knows is one who is able to, or knows how to verify the

14 Henry David Aiken, "Rationalism, Education, and the Good Society," *Studies in Philosophy and Education* 6, no. 3 (Summer, 1968): 252.
15 Ibid., p. 251.

prospositions and theories that he is said to know. In another way, scientific knowledge, which is now conceived in terms of controlled inquiry and explanation, does not consist in intuitive perceptions of the thing known, but rather in an ability to offer satisfactory explanations of it.[16]

Neorationalism (scientific liberalism) clearly meets those criteria which are said to constitute an ideology. It possesses, as noted in the last few pages, ideas about man and society. It certainly articulates goals, ideals, standards of justification, validation, and verification—especially through scientific methodology—and it is becoming the controlling conceptual framework for individual, associative, institutional, and societal action. Furthermore, the extension of scientific method[17] fulfills what we noted earlier, through Aiken (see page 96), to be one of the major criteria of an ideology: it provides the major categorical bases of interpretation through which various forms of thought and expression are construed and interrelated. Knowledge is increasingly viewed in terms of verification, and one who knows is one who is able to verify that which he claims to know, in a manner appropriate to scientific methodology and explanation. In this and other important ways, scientific liberalism is increasingly becoming the essence of the established social order. Marcuse puts it this way:

> We live and die rationally and productively. We know that destruction is the price of progress as death is the price of life, that [self] renunciation and toil are the prerequisites for gratification and joy, that business must go on, and that the alternatives are Utopian. This ideology belongs to the established social apparatus: it is a requisite for its continuous functioning. . . .[18]

[16] Ibid., p. 254.
[17] Analyzed in detail in Ch. 5.
[18] Herbert Marcuse, *One-Dimensional Man* (Boston: Beacon Press, 1964), p. 145.

Scientific liberalism, then, is accepted by virtually the whole society in which we live, and it has become the dominant theme of our culture. Scientific liberalistic norms are embedded in the whole institutional and cultural fabric of our society, and "they form a large part of its lore, prevailing intellectual and social history, [and] what it conceives to be its traditions."[19] We wish to point out, however, that these norms are not necessarily *freely* chosen by individuals, groups, or institutions. They are, for the most part, simply absorbed. The materialistic and cohesive successes of scientific liberalism reconcile opposition to it. The function of scientific liberalism's progress is to blunt our recognition of the limits of this ideology and its irrational consequences. Scientific liberalism appears to be so beneficial—for all social groups—that any contradiction of it seems neurotic, futile, or both. Marcuse says:

> The struggle for existence and the exploitation of man and nature ... [have become] evermore scientific and rational. ... Scientific management and scientific division of labor vastly increased the productivity of the economic, political, and cultural enterprise. Result: the higher standard of living. At the same time and on the same ground, this rational enterprise produced a pattern of mind and behavior which justified and absolved even the most destructive and oppressive features of the enterprise. Scientific ... rationality and manipulation are welded together into new forms of social control.[20]

SOME CONSEQUENCES WHICH
SUPPORT BUREAUTECHNOCRACY

The wide acceptance of neorationalistic, scientific liberalistic norms is reflected in the fact that science is increasingly looked upon as *the* model of human knowing and knowledge.

[19] Aiken, "Rationalism, Education, and the Good Society," p. 250.
[20] Marcuse, *One-Dimensional Man*, p. 146.

This model is now the prevailing trend in "cognitive" disciplines which were once thought to be "outside" the dominion of scientific methodology. As members of society we are increasingly persuaded, directly or indirectly, to act on and believe only that which can be empirically verified or is implicitly offered as "scientific." It is no wonder, therefore, that society at large assigns to science and scientists the place of highest intrinsic value in the order of things. As Aiken points out: "The scientists who possess this knowledge and the skills pertaining thereto, are regarded as individuals of the highest dignity and authority among those who know. Such persons, moreover, tend to be viewed by . . . [scientific liberals or bureautechnocrats] as paradigms of human excellence generally, to be emulated wherever possible, to be deferred to where not."[21]

Scientific liberals emphasize the public, objective, impersonal, and "just" character of scientific inquiry and knowledge. Such knowledge, they tell us, is within the easy reach of anyone who can master the skills required for scientific experimentation, observation, and explanation. Questions of political, social, and economic orientation are viewed as irrelevant to an individual's ability to share in the scientific enterprise, or to enjoy the benefits of scientific education.[22] The authority turned to for sanctioning knowledge, action, thought, etc., is—the scientific liberals tell us—never the authority of political, social, or economic power, or the nonrational authority of religion, but the authority of neorationalistic principles. Sidney Hook puts it this way: "If we reject the scientific method as the supreme authority in judgment of both fact and value, what can we substitute in its stead? Every alternative involves at some point an institutional authority which, historical evidence shows, lends itself to abuse, which proclaims itself to be above all interests and becomes the expression of a particular interest invested with the symbols of public

[21] Aiken, "Rationalism, Education, and the Good Society," p. 254.
[22] Ibid., p. 256.

authority."[23] In short, scientific liberal principles, we are told, have no vested interests, and therefore are held out as the necessary essence of a society which wishes to be truly democratic. "Indeed it is commonly argued that the scientific community is a perfect democracy, a society of equals, each of whom is free to confute his fellow, if he can, and everyone is pledged to subordinate his judgment to the immanent consensus of qualified scientific observers or judges."[24]

Ideally and in principle anyone is free to enter into and gain from the neorationalistic enterprise. Given the equalitarian ideal of scientific liberalism, it is held to be necessary as a dominant cultural theme in a society which preaches democracy. Other questions aside, the scientific liberal's ideal seems to overlook human difference in scientific aptitude. "Bertrand Russell, himself . . . a rationalist, has said somewhere that the difference in intellectual capacity between an Einstein and an ordinary man is hardly less great than the difference in this regard between an ordinary man and a chimpanzee."[25]

The point is that a vast number of human beings, even under what a scientific liberal might consider optimal conditions, cannot be expected to engage in, understand, or enjoy the nature and consequences of neorationalistic processes. Moreover, some persons, regardless of aptitude, simply *do not choose* neorationalistic norms. In a society wherein intellectual ability and rationality itself are measured primarily in terms of one's ability to understand the benefits of scientific liberalism, those without scientific aptitude and those who do not choose neorationalism do not enjoy equalitarian status. Roszak put it: "Within such a society, the citizen, confronted by bewildering bigness and complexity, finds it necessary to defer on all matters to those who

[23] Sidney Hook, *John Dewey: His Philosophy of Education and Its Critics* (New York: Tamiment Institute, 1959), pp. 22–23.
[24] Aiken, "Rationalism, Education, and the Good Society," p. 256.
[25] Ibid., p. 257.

know better. . . . [Bureautechnocracy is] that society in which those who govern justify themselves by appeal to technical experts who, in turn, justify themselves by appeal to scientific forms of knowledge. And beyond the authority of science, there is no appeal."[26] In short, scientific liberalism as ideology provides "little basis or support for the principles of extensive human quality and general social or political democracy."[27] The late Gordon Allport, a leading American psychologist and one of the first to warn of impending dangers in the extension of scientific methodology beyond the borders of pure sciences, had this to say about the behavioral sciences as a result of their tendency to emulate the "pure" sciences:

> Up to now the "behavioral" sciences . . . have not provided us with a picture of man capable of creating or living in a democracy. These sciences in large part have imitated the billiard ball model of physics, now of course outmoded. They have delivered into our hands a psychology of an "empty organism," pushed by drives and molded by environmental circumstances. What is small and partial, what is external and mechanical, what is early, what is peripherial and opportunistic—have received the chief attention of psychological system builders. But the theory of democracy requires also that man possess a measure of rationality, a portion of freedom, a generic conscience, appropriate ideals, and unique value . . . Man talks, laughs, feels bored, develops a culture, has a foreknowledge of death, studies theology, and strives for the improvement of his own personality. The infinitude of resulting patterns is plainly not found in creatures of instinct. For this reason we should exercise great caution when we extrapolate the assumptions, methods, and concepts of natural and biological science to our subject matter. In particular

[26] Theodore Roszak, *The Making of a Counter Culture* (Garden City, N.Y.: Doubleday, 1969), pp. 7–8.
[27] Aiken, "Rationalism, Education, and the Good Society," p. 257.

we should refuse to carry over the indifference of other sciences to the problem of individuality.[28]

Allport overlooks what is a recurrent and fundamental feature of our argument: the psychology of "an empty organism" is essential to the continued progress of bureautechnocracy. The psychology of an "empty organism" holds that this organism is pushed by drives and molded by environmental circumstances. It ignores "generic conscience," "appropriate ideals," etc., and is an appropriate psychology for a system/environment whose maintenance and growth depends upon the implantation of false needs in individuals. A physics-oriented psychology is the major intellectual apologia for bureautechnocracy.

Protestations to the contrary, scientific liberalism, bound as it is to empirical and positivistic modes of knowing and knowledge, is elitist. Everyone cannot engage in, understand, or enjoy the nature and consequences of neorationalistic principles. Some *choose* not to so participate. Much more important, however, is the fact that the power and prestige of scientific methodology is canceling out ways of knowing which do not square with the scientific paradigm of verification. The result: science and scientists enjoy more and more power and prestige; other "knowers" and "fields" of knowing garner less and less power and prestige. They are increasingly relegated to second-class citizenship. This observation would lose its sting were scientific liberalism non-ideological. More specifically, if scientific liberalistic principles were not embedded in our cultural fabric, if these principles did not constitute active and practical social roles, if neorationalistic principles were not the principal motivating determinants of our social system, then the elitism of scientific liberalism would not be so grave in its consequences. This elitist syndrome has been recognized by numerous observers: C. Wright Mills, Jules Hen-

---

[28] Gordon W. Allport, *Becoming: Basic Considerations for a Psychology of Personality* (New Haven: Yale University Press, 1955), p. 100.

ry, Vance Packard, Erich Fromm, John Kenneth Galbraith, Thomas Molnar, and Herbert Marcuse. Each of these writers speaks of an elitist group, attached to the ideological enterprise of what we call scientific liberalism, which is used to propagandize and perpetuate bureautechnocracy. In bureautechnocracy, we become a "scientific" society. Roszak reminds us, however, that

> like Kafka's K., men throughout the "developed world" become more and more bewildered dependents of inaccessible castles wherein inscrutable technicians conjure with their fate. True, the foolproof system again and again bogs down in riot or apathetic rot or the miscalculations of overextended centralization; true, the chronic obscenity of thermonuclear war hovers over it like a gargantuan bird of prey feeding off the bulk of our affluence and intelligence. But the members of the parental generation, storm-tossed by depression, war, and protracted warscare, cling fast to the technocracy for the myopic sense of prosperous security it allows. By what right would they complain against those who intend only the best, who purport to be the agents of democratic consensus, and who invoke the high rhetorical sanction of the scientific world view, our most unimpeachable mythology? How does one take issue with the parental beneficence of such technocratic Grand Inquisitors? Not only do they provide bread aplenty, but the bread is soft as floss: it takes no effort to chew, and yet is vitamin-enriched.[29]

The elite owe their position and status to scientific liberalism. They therefore have a vested interest in making it ideology and in sustaining and strengthening it as such. Contradiction of, or resistance to, scientific liberalistic principles becomes increasingly difficult, if not futile. The answer to such resistance is always suggestive of "more science, more scientific method ap-

[29] Roszak, *The Making of a Counter Culture*, p. 13.

plied to social, moral, and emotional affairs."[30] It is not surprising that one of the major functions of the elite (as indicated by Herbert Marcuse, Jules Henry, and as discussed by us) is to give more intense expression to neorationalistic norms by propagandizing about their successes and benefits. Neorationalistic management and division of labor, for example, is praised for (what it did in fact accomplish) vastly increasing the productivity of the economic and political enterprise of our society. This success is in evidence all about us, and its progress is continually charted by the increasing standard of living. What rational man could deny this success? On this basis alone, the neorationalist has little difficulty in extracting cooperation, or in gaining attachment of societal members for and to the scientific liberalistic ideology. Scientific liberalistic norms and principles, therefore, are made out to be the very embodiment of "goodness" operating for the benefit of *all* interests. As Marcuse has noted: "Under the conditions of a rising standard of living, nonconformity with . . . [scientific liberalism] appears to be socially useless, and the more so when it entails tangible economic and political disadvantages and threatens the smooth operation of the whole."[31]

Thus scientific liberalism is self-perpetuating, and militates against that type of social change which opens up alternatives to the creative and generative aspects of human nature through recognition of, and praise of, different ways of knowing and different types of knowledge. In short, scientific liberalism's potent influence in limiting acceptable forms of knowledge and the knowing process, and its great success in providing us with an increased standard of living, have created a form of life which neutralizes all contrascientific forms. Herbert Marcuse puts it this way:

[30] Thomas Molnar, *The Decline of the Intellectual* (New York: World Publishing, 1961), p. 216.
[31] Marcuse, *One-Dimensional Man*, p. 2.

Ascending modern rationalism . . . shows a striking contrast between extreme critical radicalism in scientific and philosophic method on the one hand, and an uncritical quietism in the attitude toward established and functioning social institutions. Thus Descartes *ego cogitans* was to leave the "great public bodies" untouched, and Hobbes held that "the present ought always to be preferred, maintained, and accounted best." Kant agreed with Locke in justifying revolution *if and when* it has succeeded in organizing the whole and in preventing subversion.

However, these accommodating concepts of Reason were always contradicted by the evident misery and injustice of the "great public bodies" and the effective more or less serious rebellion against them. Societal conditions existed which provoked and permitted real dissociation from the established state of affairs; a private as well as political dimension was present in which dissociation could develop into effective opposition, testing its strength and the validity of its objectives.

[With the gradual but increasing disappearance of this dimension] . . . the self-limitation of thought assumes a larger significance. The interrelation between scientific-philosophical and societal processes, between theoretical and practical Reason, asserts itself "behind the back" of the scientists and philosophers. The society bars a whole type of oppositional operations and behavior; consequently, the concepts pertaining to them are rendered illusory or meaningless. Historical transcendence appears as metaphysical transcendence, not acceptable to science and scientific thought. The operational and behavioral point of view practiced as a "habit of thought" at large, becomes the view of the established universe of discourse and action, needs and aspirations. The "cunning of Reason" works, as it so often did, in the interest of the powers that be. The insistence on operational and behavioral concepts turns against the efforts to free thought and behavior *from* the given reality and *for* the suppressed alternatives. Theoretical and practical Reason, academic and social behaviorism meet on common ground: that of an advanced society which makes scientific and technical progress into an instrument of domination.[32]

The development of an elite class, the stress on the impersonal nature of knowing and knowledge, the view that man and society constitute an environment whose value resides in the possibilities for experimentation and control, and the gradual but increasing disarmament of opposing tendencies have all contributed to the ever increasing concentration of energy, time, talent, money, etc., on an increasingly narrow and prescribed range of human knowing activities.

How much is left out or prostituted when neorationalistic principles shut out other acceptable forms of knowing and knowledge? How much is left out when neorationalistic principles are viewed as man's unique and controlling characteristics as a knowing being?

> [We forget that] ... man is also uniquely the religious animal, the being capable of grasping his own mortality, and of making something beyond his own individual existence a matter of ultimate concern. This is something that escapes the rational animal as such. Secondly, (and here I am not interested in questions of priority or rank) man is the communal animal, capable of friendship, comradeship, and the forms of love sometimes grouped under the heading of *agape*. Man, if you will, is the animal that loves: he is therefore the animal that reciprocates and needs reciprocity. At the same time, man is also the self-perfecting, self-overcoming, and self-transcending being. And this, not only in the religious or social or intellectual dimension, but in the widest sense, in the ethical or moral dimension. Now, however, another ideal comes more distinctly into view: the ideal of self-determination, of self-control, of what Kant called "giving oneself the law." The very notion of morality is impossible apart from the ideal of the individual as an autonomous agent, who assumes re-

[32] Ibid., pp. 15–16.

sponsibility for his own conduct, his own principles, his own comportment. In fact, apart from such a view of man free, personal relations among men, including above all the relations of contract and personal loyalty and love, can scarcely exist.[33]

All these very fundamental features of the human animal are either overlooked or tacitly negated when neorationalism prevails. To contemplate human beings devoid of these human characteristics is to conjure up the unthinkable. But the unthinkable is not an unlikely *real* eventuality.

In times past, the advancement of knowledge was, or appeared to be, largely the work of independent scholars and inquirers. The transmission of the knowledge, skills, and powers essential to this advancement was far more loosely organized than it is today and, as such, too often more clumsy, slow, and faulty than today. It did, nevertheless, permit a wide range of inquiries. Today, neorationalistic limits on knowing and knowledge have created a situation wherein we witness an increasing channeling of energies into a limited range of knowing patterns. The result is the increasing institutionalization of knowing and knowledge which in turn directly contributes to an interesting paradox: the rapid enlargement of our fund of knowledge, and more difficulty for greater numbers of people to have access to and act upon the increasing store of knowledge. More specifically, the prevailing tendency to regard neorationalistic norms as the only means to acceptable knowledge has resulted in a channeling of energies into a frenetic enlargement of our funded knowledge —knowledge that can be acted upon. However, the inherent elitist quality of these means to knowing makes the increased knowledge fund available to a smaller and smaller *percentage* of people. Neorationalism, in this sense, is a breeding ground for persons susceptible to the controlling influence of those who can directly participate in the neorationalistic enterprise. It is in this

[33] Aiken, "Rationalism, Education, and the Good Society," p. 267.

regard, also, that neorationalism, hence scientific liberalism, supports and is mirrored in bureautechnocracy. As Aiken says:

> The exponential enlargement of human learning is itself a
> direct function of the development of modern institutions of
> controlled experimental inquiry. These corporate bodies, with
> their own indispensible divisions of labor, involve differential
> and stratified intellectual responsibilities and prerogatives. In
> the great scientific laboratories, for example, section heads,
> laboratory technicians, secretarial aides, and the rest are, in
> practice, organized in a quasi-platonic manner, under the di-
> rection of administrative "guardians" who at once set the
> goals for inquiry and determine the rights of various classes
> of scientific workers.[34]

The increased bureaucratization of knowing and knowledge
is a logical consequence of the scientific liberal ideology. If the
"good" is equated with neorationalism, and if the advancement
of neorationalistic patterns of knowing and knowledge is the
best of the human goods, "then in the modern world that good
must be regarded, progressively and ideally, as the collective
achievement of highly organized . . . institutions or hierarchy of
institutions."[35] Furthermore, if the scientific liberal community
is regarded as the paradigm of democracy, then scientific liberalism must be, as it is, increasingly committed to a corporate or
collectivist conception of the ideal society.

> This suggests . . . that old-fashioned libertarian notions of free
> thought and inquiry should be radically qualified, if indeed,
> not replaced altogether, in ways that take account of the real
> social conditions of scientific research. Indeed, one can readily
> imagine that, from a rationalist point of view, the free-lance
> inquirer who investigates whatever he pleases, in accordance
> with whatever procedures and standards of truth and mean-

[34] Ibid., p. 261.
[35] Ibid.

ing he may consider appropriate, is to be viewed as intellectually irresponsible and hence socially undesirable.[36]

Clearly, therefore, scientific liberalistic ideology emphasizes the notion that the rights of individual men, as rational men, as rational beings, are essentially *social rights* as defined neorationalistically or scientifically. The social man, hence the neorationalistic man, is the "good" man. The anticollectivist, the private man, the heretic, by definition opts to be such. He can choose to accept or reject neorationalism. On the other hand, neorationalism builds into important social processes and systems certain check-point devices which, while embodying the norms of neorationalism, serve as weeding-out procedures for rejecting those who cannot or will not participate in the scientific liberalistic mentality.

> [Scientific liberalism] exudes its mentality at the points where social relationships meet and important decisions are made. Family love, business activity, academic achievement, determine of course the nature of human ties in the situation of the family, business transactions, colleges; but we take it increasingly for granted that at the important checking points of all these institutions, mental-mechanical devices are set up to regulate social traffic and individual destiny. Psychological tests are administered in schools, business corporations, the army, and even in certain ecclesiastical orders. Whatever we think of these tests—and the overwhelming evidence shows that they are wretched but pretentious fumblings with an immeasurable reality—they restrict and mechanize responses, and perform a selection that excludes the free, the imaginative, the morally and socially rebellious. In the family, at law courts, in civil positions, the sense of responsibility is attacked at its roots when the so-called expert is called in to weigh love, guilt, or competence by extrarational factors, that is, by a psychological and social "science" the data and conclusions of which change

[36] Ibid.

with every rising day. The resistance of common sense is undermined by elusive but ubiquitous persons in key positions who find it easy to shock the unsuspecting "layman" (nonspecialist) into a panicky reappraisal of all that experience, example, and tradition have taught him.[37]

Such checkpoint devices not only serve to intensify and protect the extension of scientific methodology into the most mundane of human affairs while negating "nonscientific" ways of knowing and knowledge; they also serve to create "disadvantaged" persons, "drop-outs," etc. Bureautechnocracy, through scientific liberalism, while creating an aristocracy of power, while resisting qualitative change, and while insuring its own continued existence, becomes the breeding ground for societal "misfits." The hippies, the yippies, the beats, the dope culture, our unhappy workers, the organization men, the "disadvantaged" whites, blacks, and browns all have something in common: bureautechnocracy, among other things, is their enemy.

We have made recurrent reference to the fact that bureautechnocracy insures its existence and continued growth through, among other things, the widespread extension of scientific methodology. We will turn our attention to this extension in the following chapter by examination of the major element in this extension, scientific explanation.

[37] Molnar, *The Decline of the Intellectual*, p. 216.

CHAPTER 5

Closure Through Extension

SCIENTIFIC EXPLANATION

The reach of bureautechnocracy's tentacles is extended and supported by the increasingly widespread acceptance, conscious or otherwise, of the scientific liberalistic ideology. The ideology enjoys this position as a result, largely, of the extension of scientific methodology into areas where its competence is in question. Our criticisms here are not aimed at the methodology per se, but at its extension into unfamiliar fields of study and certain areas of human activity. This extension is largely a result of the wide acceptance of scientific explanation as *the* mode for explaining phenomena, be they in the physical, social, or behavioral sciences. The application of this mode of explanation to phenomena outside the "pure" sciences is the major reason, we believe, for the generation of dangerous notions regarding human nature and its control. Furthermore, this form of explanation for human behavior, attitudes, or institutional arrangements is now recognized as the principal accomplice of the anti-man culture of bureautechnocracy.

Science is concerned with linking things and events in sche-mata of cause-effect relationships. These relationships hold the key to acceptable knowledge and, hence, defensible truth. This has been the generally accepted notion of what scientific expla-nation is all about since the work of David Hume. Singular events or facts are unimportant in themselves. They become significant only as they contribute to generalizations or laws that explicatively account for all levels of relationships in the church-dom of scientific knowledge. MacIver put it this way:

> Science is interested in how things belong together, and it studies and classifies resemblances and differences from this point of view. Everything from a galaxy to an atom is con-ceived as system, as system beyond system and system with-in system. Let us go one step further—let us make explicit the hypothesis that at once vitalizes the scientific pursuit and finds progressive support in all scientific achievement, namely, the hypothesis that *things belong together in systems because it is their nature to do so*. When we have taken this step we have reached the causal significance of the relations the knowledge of which is scientific knowledge.[1]

The main business of science is, clearly, to abstract what is common among the phenomena it studies. Scientific explana-tion is the means to this end, and it is guided by the scientific assumption that phenomena are determined (caused by the action or presence of antecedent phenomena) and that the prior determining causes fix exactly what the consequential effect shall be. This is especially true of the physical sciences and is true of the behavioral and social sciences when they emulate (as is increasingly the case) the explicative model of the physi-cal sciences.

A scientific explanation of a phenomenon, be it in the "pure"

[1] R. M. MacIver, *Social Causation* (New York: Harper and Row Torch-books, 1964), pp. 98–99.

sciences or in the behavioral and social sciences, becomes defensible truth or scientific knowledge to the extent that it can be verified. In terms of scientific explanation, the test of defensible truth is empirical verification. "If science is to tell us anything about the world . . . it must somewhere contain empirical elements. . . . For it is by experience alone that information about the world is received."[2] Basically, a scientific explanation is empirically verified when it is publicly tested and is shown to be an effective basis for prediction and control. In the words of David Hume, statements purporting to explain phenomena which cannot be empirically verified should be committed "to the flames: for . . . [they] contain nothing but sophistry and illusion."[3]

To say that science is concerned only with that which is open to public verification does not mean that it necessarily denies that which does not fit its explicative pattern and criteria of defensible truth. Science does not deny, for example, the existence and occurrence of purposive or intentional behavior, and all that goes with such behavior—self, value, freedom, subjectivity. However, these matters cannot be verified by scientific method, and no matter how widespread may be the "belief" that they exist and occur, they carry the stigma of being nonobjective. Furthermore, *knowledge* of these matters is impossible, since knowledge (in the scientific sense) is only that which is empirically verifiable.

Scientific explanation cannot show concern for the individual or the singular. Science—as its mode of explanation makes clear —is aimed at linking phenomena under general laws or principles, with harmonizing all things, and with predicting the behavior of that which it subsumes under general laws. For several reasons, individuals, or singular facts or events, are less important than the group, collectivity, or series of events; some-

---

[2] Abraham Kaplan, *The Conduct of Inquiry: Methodology for Behavioral Science* (San Francisco: Chandler, 1964), p. 34.

[3] As quoted in Gerard De Gre, *Science as a Social Institution* (New York: Random House, 1955), p. 18.

times the individual cannot be reached, and other times the individual would seemingly destroy the pattern sought after.

> In this connection, we may refer to the well known Heisenberg indeterminancy principle. Roughly stated, the principle holds that the path of an individual electron is unpredictable, because the process of observation itself affects the behavior of the phenomena under investigation. This observation underlines the probability character of modern physics. At the same time, the unpredictability of the behavior of a single electron in no way destroys the possibility of arriving at physical generalizations. For although individual electrons may behave unpredictably, a population of electrons in an atomic field structure performs with a very high degree of statistical regularity, which makes it possible to arrive at physical laws of a sufficient degree of probability to closely approximate unity. The generalizing sciences deal at all times with such collective phenomena, and with the probable patterns of behavior of populations, whether of electrons, fruit flies, or human beings.[4]

This statement tells us that though the individual electron may be unique, its uniqueness is not important vis-à-vis the group of electrons. By default, the uniqueness of the individual electron is negated. The tendency to overlook the individual, as illustrated in this statement, is not missing in the behavioral and social sciences. Science, because of its explanation patterns, is interested in collective phenomena. And this is the case in the "human" sciences as well as in the physical.

The widespread authority and prestige of scientific methodology, reflected in and enhanced by its extension into fields outside the "pure sciences," have successfully turned the inquirer's attention away from the nonempirically verifiable, the unique, the particular, the unpredictable. We slight the fact that man is the only being capable of making something beyond his own

[4] Ibid., p. 40.

individual existence a matter of ultimate concern. We treat lightly the fact that man is a social animal capable of love and all the concomitants which follow from this capacity. We overlook man's self-determining possibilities. In short, the extension of scientific methodology, with its unique pattern of explanation and the aims attendant thereto, has resulted in a diminished concern for those aspects of man which do not fit the explicative pattern but which, ironically, are some of the hallmarks of man as man.

Scientific knowledge is always offered as tentative, open to change, and intolerant of absolutism. But testimony such as this loses its meaning in light of the fact that the knowledge-getting process of science is becoming a virtual absolute. More specifically, the criteria of scientific knowledge, hence defensible truth, as evidenced in the pattern of explanation, have become the criteria of all knowledge; other forms and processes of knowing are implicitly denied. This is evidenced in the increasing influence of scientific methodology and its assumptions in psychology, sociology, philosophy, and other fields of study. Problems and questions related to matters which grow out of human subjectivity and personal knowledge are looked upon as pseudo problems, not worthy of intellectual consideration, or problems which ought to be looked upon as another form of objective, i.e., scientifically treatable, problem. One sociologist, discussing the role of scientific explanation, reveals this latter outlook: "Political and social upheavals . . . such as wars, revolutions, and crime are to most people a matter of shock and much personal recrimination and other emotionalism. Yet these societal events are 'natural' in the same sense that 'physical' events are 'natural.' 'Natural' and 'physical' are of course merely words by which we describe a relatively objective (corroborated) type of adjustment to the phenomena so designated."[5]

[5] George Lundberg, "The Postulates of Science and Their Implicatons for Sociology," in Maurice Natanson, ed., *Philosophy of the Social Sciences: A Reader* (New York: Random House, 1963), p. 39.

The author of this statement forgets to mention the role of language in shaping thought and perception. More important, however, is the fact that he is proselytizing about, and perpetuating, one of the logical by-products of a pervasive scientific ethic: "Science and everything scientific can be and often is used as a tool in the service of a distorted, narrowed, humorless, de-eroticized, de-emotionalized, desacralized and desanctified *Weltanschauung*. This desacralization can be used as a defense against being flooded by emotion, especially the emotions of humility, reverence, mystery, wonder, and awe.[6]

The extension of scientific methodology into the study of human nature and behavior is completely consistent with the requirements of bureautechnocracy. The widespread extension and influence of scientific methodology "serves to coordinate ideas and goals with those exacted by the . . . [bureautechnocratic] system, to enclose them in the system, and to repel those which are irreconcilable with the system."[7] This results in man's increasing dependence on things outside himself; a turn away from things subjective to a dependence on the "objective order of things"—on economic laws, collective opinion, the demands of the marketplace.

The interdependency of science and bureautechnocracy should not be too surprising. The course that science takes has always been tied in to the socioeconomic system of which it is a part.[8] In bureautechnocracy, we find that the neorationalistic flavor of the marketplace finds its counterpart in the neorationalism of scientific methodology. Our government encourages the extension of science. Industry learns that funds put into "scientific" research, be it chemical research or marketing psychology, pay off with handsome dividends. Our colleges and

---

[6] Abraham Maslow, *The Psychology of Science* (New York: Harper and Row, 1966), p. 139.

[7] Herbert Marcuse, *One-Dimensional Man* (Boston: Beacon Press, 1964), p. 14.

[8] See, for example, De Gre, *Science as a Social Institution*.

universities clearly support the extension of science; their alliance with government and industry on myriad mutually satisfying scientific projects create powerful combined forces for the extension of science. Finally, "the control of nature as the end of science [is echoed in] the control of community and economy brought about by . . . [bureautechnocracy and the rule of laws associated with it]."[9]

MAN AS OBJECT UNTO HIMSELF

The extension of scientific methodology into what are now called the human sciences explains how the extension of scientific methodology at large supports bureautechnocracy. It was necessary to develop a conception of man which would permit him to become an object of scientific knowledge, an object unto himself. The extension of scientific methodology rests on the assumption that the "methods in scientific investigation . . . [apply] to *all* branches of science and not only to the physical sciences."[10] But, beyond this, what was needed was a conception of man compatible with the means and aims of scientific inquiry. In the behavioral and social sciences, this need has largely been satisfied. Man has been reconceived in such a way that inquiry into his conduct, and conclusions reached by such inquiry, could be made to fit the pattern of defensible truth in the empirical sense. Certain things about man as an object of study had to be ignored, while some things would have to be given high priority. Highest on the priority list was that of overt behavior or that which could be reducible to some kind of quantification; with this arena as his major focus, the student of man applying scientific techniques to the object of his study (man) would be operating in a realm which lends itself to the pattern of scientific

9 Ibid., p. 16.
10 Philip H. Phenix, *Realms of Meaning* (New York: McGraw-Hill, 1964), p. 102. Italics ours.

explanation. Here the student of man could employ evidential statements, relate them to generalizations, and reach conclusions which are open to the test of public verification.

The word *science*, in the lexicon of the "pure" sciences, relates to knowledge of the external world. Applying this to man means treating man as an object unto himself. Humans are to be studied as objects "out there." In individual human terms, this means, among other things, "looking at something that is not you, not human, not personal, something independent of you the perceiver. It is something to which you are a stranger, a bystander, a member of the audience. You the observer are, then, really alien to it, uncomprehending and without sympathy and identification, without any starting point of tacit knowledge that you might already have."[11]

Scientific explanation, as we have already noted, is aimed at generalization: identifying parallel processes of development and action that can be traced to particular origins or causes and subsumed under a general law or principle. In this way, certain phenomena under study can be classified, organized and structured, "simplifying huge numbers of separate instances, even infinite numbers of them. [Generalization] . . . does not refer to any one experience or to any one thing or object, but to categories or kinds of things or experiences."[12] Accordingly, man as phenomenon had to be classified or categorized within a system so as to meet the demands of scientific explanation; namely, the procedures called for in deducing generalizations about particulars within a system. This requirement was to be accounted for in a conception of man which is generally known as the *reductionist* point of view.

This view operates from the premise that man, in the order of all things, is nothing more than a highly complex physiochemical system, of the same kind as lower forms of life but more complicated. We are told that nothing essential is lost in study-

[11] Maslow, *The Psychology of Science*, p. 49.
[12] Ibid., p. 80.

ing the simpler forms of life as deductive models, because man is of the same system. Furthermore, the methods used in the study of lower forms of life are held out, by this point of view, as appropriate for the "scientific" study of man. "Rat" psychology and its method are not inappropriate for a human psychology. The sociology of communal animals—ants, bees, buffalo, etc.—is held to offer modes of inquiry and substantive knowledge appropriate to the sociological study of man. Labeled by some as the doctrine of the "empty organism," this conception made way for the use of scientific methodology in the study of man; a workable conception was now provided which asserted that there is no difference in *kind* between the lower animals and man, but only a difference in *degree* of complexity. "The hypothesis of the 'empty organism' or 'hollow man,' along with the belief that the higher animals, including man, are essentially similar in fundamental nature, has led to the view that man's nature can be known by means of studies of lower species of animals. If man is merely an animal, then investigations of simpler animals, such as the white rat or the guinea pig, will reveal man's nature."[13]

By itself, the reductionist position is not at issue. We have learned from it that, biologically, "man is not different in kind from other forms of life; that living matter is not different in kind from dead matter; and therefore man is an assembly of atoms that obeys natural laws of the same kind that a star does."[14] All of this has been made quite clear in the last few years, "first by the elucidation of the atomic architecture of the hereditary material in man, and then by recent progress in analyzing the electrical and chemical processes in the brain."[15] The *implications* of the reductionist position, however, prove dangerously misleading. Nothing is said about man as *a* person. Many behav-

13 Harold Titus, *Living Issues in Philosophy*, 4th ed. (New York: American Book Company, 1964), p. 153.
14 Jacob Bronowski, *The Identity of Man* (Garden City, N.Y.: Natural History Press, 1966), p. 8.
15 Ibid.

ioral and social scientists who adopt this point of view rule out
concerns with *a* person as trivial and unscientific. "Practically
all scientists (of the impersonal) proceed on the tacit or explicit
assumption that one studies classes or groups of things, not single
things. Of course you actually look at one thing at a time, one
paramecium, one piece of quartz, one particular kidney, one
schizophrenic. But each one is treated as a sample of a species
or a class, and therefore as interchangeable."[16]

Given the lack of concern with the personal and individual,
and the emphasis on that which is quantifiable, we should not
be surprised that the reductionist position—and, largely, the
"scientific" approach to the study of man—is not concerned
with the self, wherein the self somehow relates to the individual's perception of his being as the central point of all his
relationships.

B. F. Skinner, perhaps the leading American behavioral psychologist, has said in this regard that since *self* is a scientifically
meaningless term, we have reason to reject it and its notion.
Some biologists, on the other hand, intrigued by the human
body's rejection reaction to transplanted organs through the
build-up of certain body chemicals, "have taken to using the
word *self* to mean the set of my body chemicals, and *not-self* to
mean another set. They say that the self recognizes and respects
itself, and rejects what is not self."[17]

In defining self in empirical terms, and by ignoring or ruling
out the personal, the reductionist scientific conception provided
the necessary bridge to allow for the extension of scientific
methodology to the study of man. In several ways the conception, which is merely premise, has become conclusion.[18] Science
considers

[16] Maslow, *The Psychology of Science*, pp. 8–9.
[17] Bronowski, *The Identity of Man*, p. 11.
[18] We recognize that there has been a resurgence within the discipline of
   psychology of the existential approach to psychological inquiry. We
   also recognize that what Maslow has called the third force in psychology
   —emphasis on *interpersonal* knowledge—has gained some momentum

the universe and man in it as an *environment*, whose infinite transformability is an end in itself. In this view, human consciousness is merely a (temporarily) privileged location for sizing up the rest of the universe, but neither the most perfect, nor possessing any intrinsic value. The goal is to spread the consciousness over the universe, to identify and equalize mind and matter (monism) and to set up other stations of ideation and control. Such intentions are evident in the work of scientists who reduce the activities of the human mind to the reflexes of animals.[19]

What this means is that man is viewed as lacking intrinsic worth—that he is not an end unto himself. He is, rather, valuable only in the sense that he can be experimented with, changed, and reduced to generalized laws which fit him into a grand scheme. In short, we are told that the activities of the human mind, though more complex, can be reduced to the reflexes of animals and, accordingly, that man can be stripped of emotions and instincts, and studied as if he did not have any.

It must be recognized that the study of man without the delimitations of the assumptions of scientific explanation and the reductionist conception might very well lead to the scientifically *meaningless*; this does not mean, however, that one is led to the realm of the meaningless per se. Nevertheless, we are increasingly unwilling to consider as meaningful conclusions, ideas, or thoughts about man as man which do not fit the pattern of scientific inquiry and explanation. This unwillingness, of course, is traceable to the reductionist classification of man. We have categorized man, and the categorization allows for only certain types of inquiries and conclusions. What we fail to recognize, however, is that the categorizing has resulted in a category mis-

---

during recent years. Nevertheless, these approaches hold little attraction in pschology writ large, and they have little impact upon psychological study which is aimed at controlling and predicting man's behavior.

[19] Thomas Molnar, *The Decline of the Intellectual* (New York: World Publishing, 1961), p. 212.

take: representing facts about one thing as if they belong to another. Gilbert Ryle's illustration of a category mistake may be helpful here:

> A foreigner visiting Oxford or Cambridge for the first time is shown a number of colleges, libraries, playing fields, museums, scientific departments and administrative offices. He then asks, "But where is the University? I have seen where the members of the College live, where the Registrar works, where the scientists experiment and the rest. But I have not yet seen the University in which reside and work the members of your University." It has then to be explained to him that the University is not another collateral institution, some ulterior counterpart to the colleges, laboratories and offices which he has seen. The University is just the way in which all that he has already seen is organized. When they are seen and when their coordination is understood, the University has been seen. His mistake lay in his innocent assumption that it was correct to speak of Christ Church, the Bodleian Library, the Ashmolean Museum *and* the University, to speak, that is, as if "the University" stood for an extra member of the class of which these other units are members. He was mistakenly allocating the University to the same category as that to which the other institutions belong.[20]

In terms of our discussion, the categorizing of man in the reductionist framework may be a category mistake of the kind illustrated above. The workable, reductionist conception categorizes man and paves the way for study of him as a sample. Conclusions or ideas about man as man which do not come through scientific explanation, and which do not follow from a reductionist conception, are outside the scientifically meaningful category and are negated. But, as with the university in Ryle's illustration, man as man loses his singular identity. "Any one

[20] Gilbert Ryle, *The Concept of Mind* (New York: Barnes and Noble, 1949), p. 16.

sample is just that, a sample; it is not itself. It stands for something. It is anonymous, expendable, not unique, not sacred, not *sine qua non*; it has no proper name all its own and is not worthwhile in itself as a particular instance. It is interesting only insofar as it represents something other than itself."[21] In short, the reduction of things and events to systems, classes, and categories involves for all things so reduced, including man, a destruction of individuality and identity.

The social scientist's concern is the physical, observable, measurable side of man. He is not—*he cannot be*—interested in matters which are viewed as subjective aspects of existence and, hence, as scientifically meaningless and outside the realm of "knowledge." If the various subjective phenomena (self, valuing, loving, feeling) are used or discussed at all, they are employed within conceptual schemes suitable to those for explaining observable phenomena. For example, anger would not be explained in terms of subjective states of experience, but in terms of biochemical changes, facial expressions, and other bodily gestures, such as increase in body temperature. (In this fashion, the behavioral sciences,[22] as examples, accommodate scientific methodology and lay claim to being "objective" and "scientific" with observable phenomena as their most fundamental concept.)

[21] Maslow, *The Psychology of Science*, p. 9.

[22] Sociology especially has felt the invasion of the scientific methodology. Avoidance of explanatory concepts which account for subjective experience (a "need" of scientific explanation) is the major reason why individual thought and action are ignored, discredited, or negated when the social scientist explains social phenomena. Because of the demands scientific explanation places upon him, the social scientist "never looks for a background of mature judgments, conscious preferences, hesitations and doubts, the interplay of clear concepts within the individual mind and the willingness of others to be convinced by arguments or their freedom to refuse such; he invariably seeks psychological or sociological motives (that is, factors that are outside of the individual's sphere of consciousness and action), speaks of indoctrination and 'internalization,' stresses behavioral signs and favors the technique of anonymity" (Thomas Molnar, *The Decline and Fall of the Intellectual*, pp. 214–15).

Subjective phenomena, when they have to be considered, are typically related to external material factors as effect to cause; they are "bent" to accommodate the explicative pattern. What is emotion? A response of the involuntary muscles to external stimuli. What is speech? Movement of the throat muscles. A more "sophisticated" approach, much in evidence in contemporary philosophizing, is exemplified in the following statement by Brennan, who, in discussing this development in philosophy, notes that "ethical values . . . [emerge] from the desire of the organism to preserve its life and well-being. Aesthetic values arise from the need on the part of the organism to release emotional tensions brought about by physiological or environmental conditions. Religious values have their origin in the fears and insecurities of a highly sensitive animal organism, frightened by physical phenomena and overborn by the enormity of the universe."[23] In the area of the emotions F. V. Smith illustrates this tendency: "Sorrow, for example, might be designated by failure to enter into various social undertakings and lack of zest in activities which are usually associated with zest. Facial expression . . . could be related to some of the general features of the personality and the typical style of behavior of the individual."[24]

One can see that these examples of "how to account for subjective aspects of existence" (and behavior) do not deny that human beings act on values. However, as subjective aspects of experience, they must be either ignored or manipulated to fit the scientific pattern. In the eyes of the scientifically influenced student of man, behavior—that which is observable—is more important than ideas. The opposition to admitting anything subjective—apart from that which can be made to "fit" the necessary explicative pattern as illustrated in the above examples—has

[23] Joseph G. Brennan, *The Meaning of Philosophy* (New York: Harper and Row, 1953), p. 238.
[24] F. V. Smith, *Explanation of Human Behavior*, 2nd ed. (London: Constable and Company, 1960), p. 367.

contributed to the belief that whatever is physical, external, tangible, and measurable is more fundamental and important than that which is not.

The "scientifically" influenced student of man treats man as a phenomenon "out there"—a phenomenon to be analyzed in a manner that is no different in kind from studying or analyzing the rat in a maze. He looks at man as through a microscope,

> a keyhole, peering, peeping, from a distance, from outside, not as one who has the right to be in the room being peeped into. Such a scientific observer is not a participant observer. His science can be likened to a spectator sport, and he to a spectator. He has no necessary involvement with what he is looking at, no loyalties, no stake in it. He can be cool, detached, emotionless, desireless, wholly other than what he is looking at. He is in the grandstand looking down upon the goings-on in the arena; he himself is not in the arena. And ideally he doesn't care who wins.[25]

It logically follows that attention—in the "scientific" study of man—is focused upon that which is caused or determined and, hence, not free. It is not surprising, therefore, that many people, without hesitation, draw the conclusion that human freedom is an illusion, if "freedom" means the exemption of any part of our behavior from derivative physical laws.[26] In one sense, we do not need B. F. Skinner to remind us of the following; we already sense it: "The hypothesis that man is *not* free is essential to the application of scientific method to the study of human behavior. The free inner man who is held responsible for the behavior of the external biological organism is only a pre-scientific substitute for the kinds of causes which are discovered in the course

---

[25] Maslow, *The Psychology of Science*, pp. 49–50.

[26] There is an interesting philosophical irony in the fact that while science is based primarily upon reason and free inquiry, the conception of man necessary for this method to be applied to him stresses man's lack of freedom and the "causes" which determine his behavior.

of a scientific analysis. All these alternative causes lie *outside* the individual."[27]

The pattern of scientific explanation does not and cannot account for man as a *free self*, a being who wishes to be, and is, different from others, who can and does act in unexpected ways, and can and does choose his own direction.

The view that self, however defined, does not exist has a long history in philosophy. In the sixth century B.C., the founder of Buddhism, Siddharta Gautuama—called the Buddha or the "Enlightened One"—contended that all things are impermanent and thereby gave rise to the doctrine of "no-self." Up to this point, self had been tied in with an immortal, nonmaterial entity, the soul. This doctrine (open to various interpretations) came to be stressed in the Hinaynna form of Buddhism. David Hume was the early spokesman in the Western tradition of the doctrine of "no-self," and it was he who provided the early intellectual foundation for the bridging of the extension of scientific methodology from the "pure sciences" to the behavioral and social sciences. Others have followed this lead in denying the self, at least in any sense in which the term has been used by philosophers. Today, for instance, we find the high priest of behavioral psychology in America (Skinner) speaking of man as a machine, and asserting that a "concept of self is not essential in an analysis of behavior." In addition, he tells us that "since mental or psychic behavior . . . lacks the dimension of physical science, we have an additional reason for rejecting them."[28]

THE INTERDEPENDENCY OF
SCIENCE AND BUREAUTECHNOCRACY

Bureautechnocracy, as a culture, is built upon this logic. The terms we have used to describe the nature and consequences

[27] B. F. Skinner, *Science and Human Behavior* (New York: Macmillan, 1953), p. 47.
[28] Ibid., p. 48.

of bureautechnocracy are not unlike those we have used to describe the nature and consequences of the extension of science. Science sustains bureautechnocracy; it increasingly dominates our way of thinking. In our bureautechnocratic environment, bureaucracy, technology, scientific method, behaviorism, and reductionism all meet on common ground: "that of an advanced society which makes scientific and technical progress into an instrument of domination."[29] The term *progress* is not a neutral term. Progress suggests movement in certain directions or toward certain ends; the directions are reflective of choices, hence some value base. Today, we tend to limit progress to scientific or technical change. In a very real sense, we have come to look upon science as the only *agent* of progress. This restricted view of progress is a good operating position or principle for bureautechnocracy because science, the mainspring of this system, is also the chief means of perfecting control of means of action. In this way, the only check on science is more science. In this sense, therefore, science becomes end as well as means. This is the end of dialectics. This notion of progress protects the system from fundamental change. It becomes a way of avoiding alternatives and, perhaps most important, it serves to relieve anxiety.

Science is the mainspring of bureautechnocracy. Science is held out as the chief agent of progress. The only check on science is more science. This being the case, any anxiety generated by the system is repressed through faith in science as means to the good life. Furthermore, scientific rhetoric suggests the opposite of anxiety. The "nice" scientific words of science, "prediction," "control," "rigor," "certainty," "exactness," "preciseness," "neatness," "order," "proof," "reliability," "organization," "lawfulness," and "efficiency" are psychically soothing. But as Maslow says, they "are all capable of being pathologized when pushed to the extreme. All of them may be pressed into the service of the safety needs, i.e., they may become primarily anxiety-avoiding and anxiety-controlling mechanisms . . . for detoxifying a chaotic and

[29] Marcuse, *One-Dimensional Man*, p. 16.

frightening world."[30] In short, some of the language of science may lead us to believe (may even be *used* to make us believe) that the world is "orderly," "lawful," etc.

The prevailing notion of progress and its controlling agent, science, can therefore be ways of avoiding life. Science is increasingly performing a conserving, defensive function. We use it to blunt the oppressive features of our society by using its findings in the creation and manipulation of false needs. We fall upon science to show us the way to organize and control people. We use it as a crutch by saying that science will continue to find better ways to get us out of areas perceived as problems. In short, science, a tool, has become symbol, and the symbol, principle. We have made the fatal mistake of allowing means to become ends. The great danger with which we are now faced is that the enterprise of science has become so functionally interdependent with bureautechnocracy that they have become "a kind of Chinese Wall against innovation, creativeness, revolution, even against new truth itself if it is too upsetting."[31]

In Chapter One, we cited some examples of the way in which bureautechnocracy resists qualitative change. Time and space do not permit an extended discussion of the way in which science and bureautechnocracy, as functionally interdependent systems of thought and organization, combine to form a "Chinese Wall against innovation." But perhaps one good illustration will make the point. The modes of operation of Synanon, Alcoholics Anonymous, and other like groups provide excellent examples. These groups operate on the *belief* that only a cured drug addict or alcoholic can fully appreciate, understand, communicate with, help, and cure other addicts or alcoholics. "Only the one who *knows* is accepted at all by addicts. Addicts permit themselves to be known only by addicts. Furthermore, only addicts passionately want to cure addicts. Nobody else loves them enough and understands them enough. As they themselves say, 'Only some-

[30] Maslow, *The Psychology of Science*, p. 30.
[31] Ibid., p. 33.

body who has been through the same mill really *knows.*' "[32] It is generally accepted that the Synanon type of therapy cures many addicts. On the other hand,

> our whole apparatus of hospitals, physicians, police, prisons, psychiatrists, and social workers cures practically none. But this ineffective and perhaps worse than useless apparatus has the complete support of the whole society, of all the professions, and eats up huge amounts of money. The effective method . . . gets practically no money at all, no official support, and indeed, it is officially neglected or opposed by all the professions, by the government, by the foundations.[33]

The success of the Synanon treatment appears to go beyond scientific explanation as such—the main reason perhaps for its lack of support from society at large. What we see in the Synanon illustration is the absurdity of bureautechnocratic resistance to change which calls for altering the system's apparatus and way of thinking. What we have here is a case "in which truth is really true only when gathered by properly certified and uniformed 'truth collectors' and according to traditionally sanctified methods or ceremonies."[34]

Recent obituaries eulogizing the death of ideology have failed to recognize the potent influence of the scientific mentality as our new mental prop. Behavioral scientists seem to take it for granted that the findings of their science will be used in predicting and controlling human behavior; B. F. Skinner has been quite clear in admonishing psychologists to use the powers of control which their discipline provides. He believes:

> We must accept the fact that some kind of control of human affairs is inevitable. We cannot use good sense in human affairs unless someone engages in the design and construction

[32] Ibid., pp. 58–59.
[33] Ibid., p. 60.
[34] Ibid., p. 61.

of environmental conditions which affect the behavior of man. Environmental changes have always been the condition for the improvement of cultural patterns, and we can hardly use the more effective methods of science without making changes on a grander scale. . . . Science has turned up dangerous processes and materials before. To use the facts and techniques of a science of man to the fullest extent without making some monstrous mistake will be difficult and obviously perilous. It is no time for self-deception, emotional indulgence, or the assumption of attitudes which are no longer useful.[35]

This is benign enough, but in the same article Skinner adds to it by pointing out that as scientific explanation becomes more and more comprehensive, we are forced to accept the theoretical structure and foundation with which science represents facts. What is distressing about this "forced acceptance," however, is made more explicit:

This structure [we must accept] is clearly at odds with the traditional democratic conception of man. Every discovery of an event which has a part in shaping a man's behavior seems to leave so much the less to be credited to the man himself; and as such explanations become more and more comprehensive, the contribution which may be claimed by the individual himself appears to approach zero. Man's vaunted creative powers, his original accomplishments in art, science and morals, his capacity to choose and our right to hold him responsible for the consequences of his choice—none of these is conspicuous in this new self-portrait. Man, we once believed, was free to express himself in art, music and literature, to inquire into nature, to seek salvation in his own way. He could initiate action and make spontaneous and capricious changes of course. Under the most extreme duress some sort of choice remained to him. He could resist any effort to control him, though it might cost him his life. But science insists that action is initi-

[35] B. F. Skinner, "Freedom and the Control of Man," *American Scholar* (Winter, 1955–56): 56–57.

ated by forces impinging upon the individual, and that caprice is only another name for behavior for which we have not yet found a name.[36]

And then Skinner pours salt into the wound:

> In rallying men against tryanny it was necessary that the individual be strengthened, that he be taught that he had rights and could govern himself. To give the common man a new conception of his worth, his dignity, and his power to save himself, both here and hereafter, was often the only recourse of the revolutionist. . . . [This philosophy is an obstacle today] if it prevents us from applying to human affairs the science of man.[37]

This, then, is the length to which our scientific thinking has carried us. But that is not all. Bureautechnocracy guarantees its own survival by sustaining an educational system which propagandizes the young to accept the intellectual framework of what we might call social scientism. To this we turn to Chapter Six.

[36] Ibid., pp. 52–53.
[37] Ibid., pp. 53–54.

CHAPTER 6

The Perpetuator

"What is honored in a country will be cultivated there."
—Plato

MIRROR AND CRITIC

Whenever he is asked to comment on the ills of our educational system, Robert M. Hutchins replies that nothing is wrong with the educational system per se; what is wrong, as such, is to be found in society. Hutchins argues that education as process and institution is a mirror image of the values, drives, patterns of organization and control, etc., which prevail in the larger society in which the educational system operates. "The educational system that any country has will be the system that country wants."[1]

In this chapter we shall examine the relationship between our schools[2] and what we have called bureautechnocracy. More specifically, we shall examine the interdependency between our schools and bureautechnocratic forms and processes. It is our contention that the American public school, through historical

[1] Robert M. Hutchins, *Education for Freedom* (Baton Rouge: Louisiana State University Press, 1943), p. 4.
[2] Although occasional reference will be made to private schools and institutions of higher learning, our major referent here is the American public school, K–12.

137

accident and nationalistic chauvinism, has come to serve the imperatives of bureautechnocracy while denying the human potential of its clients.

There is nothing new in the idea of the schools reflecting the aspirations of the people who build and attend them. The notion of education as "the transmission of the culture" certainly implies such a relationship. Our theocratic colonial ancestors saw to it that their children learned to read the Bible, the basal reader of the seventeenth century, in order to reach their own accommodation with God. Their eighteenth-century successors added the concerns of *this* world to the curriculum and made certain that their children learned to read, write, and cipher in order to prosper in the here and now; material and spiritual success became the twin aims of education, and the former was taken as an indicator of the latter. In the nineteenth century, people in the process of industrialization asked their schools to educate the young in the secular subjects of mathematics, history, living languages, and science, and to train them specifically for occupational skills such as "agriculture and the mechanic arts."

We should not be too surprised, therefore, to discover the American school of the twentieth century swinging with the polity, reading the dials of public preference and responding with an accommodating scholastic program. Indeed, it has been only a few years since the voices of Hyman Rickover, James Conant, and Myron Lieberman sang out loud and clear among a number of critics attempting to get American schools into *greater* accommodation with the imperatives of advanced industrialized society.[3] The implicit assumptions in their arguments were: (1) Americans have created a reasonably just and workable society; (2) education ought to imitate more closely the techno-

[3] See, for example, Hyman G. Rickover, *Education and Freedom* (New York: Dutton, 1957); James B. Conant, *Slums and Suburbs* (New York: McGraw-Hill, 1961) and *The Education of American Teachers* (New York: McGraw-Hill, 1963); Myron Lieberman, *Education as a Profession* (Englewood Cliffs, N.J.: Prentice-Hall, 1956) and *The Future of Public Education* (Chicago: University of Chicago Press, 1960).

logical know-how and efficiency of that society; (3) education ought to produce individuals who will more easily adjust to and fit into that society. These critics were arguing, therefore, for a stronger, more integrated interpendence between school and society.

However, there has always run parallel to the "transmit the culture" theory of education another countervailing obligation by the school to "criticize the culture," to sift out the meaner elements and to further the nobler sentiments and impulses of the wider population. This obligation is implicit in the very creation of the educational profession, a cadre of individuals specifically singled out to care for the upbringing of the young and to make sure that their development represents the best qualities of the older members of the culture. Our argument in the present volume is that the school of the twentieth century has forfeited this critical role and has been seduced and captured by the bureautechnocratic ethos. If Plato is right that "what is honored in a country will be cultivated there," the question remains: What is honored? If the answer is science and bureautechnocracy, then the schools have remained true to their service role. But if the answer is individual dignity and personal development, then we are witnessing in American education a miscarriage of the "critique" function which every educator is expected to bring to his work.

By way of illustrating such a miscarriage, we offer the following commentary on three developments in American education which have, rather without our realizing it, taken over our schools and crowded out individualism and personal identity in our children. We refer to (1) the "melting pot" ideology, (2) education and scientific liberalism, and (3) education and bureaucracy.

THE "MELTING POT" IDEOLOGY

The American public school has often been eulogized for its assimilative power, the ability to "Americanize" the different

ethnic groups which it serves. The assimilative function in American education came into its own as a "melting pot" theory during the early decades of the twentieth century, the era of mass
immigration. It was the general belief during this period that the
immigrants must divest themselves of a variety of Old World
and ethnic traditions if they were to become Americanized.
This belief was so pervasive, and our schools were so successful
in implementing it in educational practice, that the immigrants
themselves internalized it, warning their children to forget their
cultural past and to copy the attitudes and behaviors of their
American school chums. The public school was the most effective agent in applying this pressure. Foreign-born children were
punished in several different ways if they showed any resistance
to assimilative demands. Those who refused to submit either
found themselves forced out of school, or they took the escape
route of dropping out.

A great deal of sentimentalism has surrounded this politico-
educational phenomenon. Henry Steele Commager has written
in lavish rhetoric that the American public school, certainly not
without its faults, is nevertheless remarkable for its astounding
achievement in bringing millions of aliens into the mainstream
of American life through the medium of homogenizing widely
different culture patterns and value systems into a common
"American" outlook.

John Dewey, often called the father of modern education, saw
the school's assimilative function as good and necessary. In
Democracy and Education he wrote:

> It is the office of the school environment to balance the various
> elements in the social environment, and to see to it that each
> individual gets an opportunity to escape from the limitations
> of the social group in which he was born, and to come into
> living contact with a broader environment. . . . With the de-
> velopment of commerce, transportation, intercommunication,
> and emigration, countries like the United States are composed
> of a combination of different groups with different traditional

customs. It is this situation which has, perhaps more than any other one cause, forced the demand for an educational institution which shall provide something like a homogeneous and balanced environment for the young. Only in this way can the centrifugal forces set up by juxtaposition of different groups within one and the same political unit be counteracted.[4]

Here, says Dewey, the school exercises its liberating function, enabling the individual to escape the accident of birth into a given social or ethnic group. The school also serves the interests of society by providing culturally different immigrants with a common frame of reference.

The assimilative function, called necessary by Dewey and praised by Commager, is a function of what is perceived as a "good" and necessary convergence of the interests of the individual and society. For example, Theodore Roosevelt's 1919 prescription for dealing with what Dewey antiseptically called "the centrifugal forces set up by the juxtaposition of different groups":

> There must be no sagging back in the fight for Americanism merely because the war is over. . . . Our principle in this matter should be absolutely simple. In the first place, we should insist that if the immigrant who comes here in good faith becomes an American and assimilates himself to us, he shall be treated on an exact equality with everyone else. But this is predicated upon the man's becoming in very fact an American and nothing but an American. . . . There can be no divided allegiance here. . . . We have room for but one flag, the American flag. . . . We have room for but one language here, and that is the English language, for we intend to see that the crucible turns out people as Americans. . . . and not as dwellers in a polyglot boarding house.[5]

[4] John Dewey, *Democracy and Education* (New York: Macmillan, 1916), pp. 24–25.
[5] Theodore Roosevelt, "Keep up the Fight for Americanism," *El Grito: A Journal of Contemporary Mexican-American Thought* 1, no. 2, p. 5.

The "melting pot" common school became a "crucible" as postwar America resumed its prewar reaction against the "new migration" of eastern and southern Europeans begun in the late 1880's. In the Chicago of 1919, according to Carl Sandburg (then a newspaper reporter), the flames of postwar "Americanization" in the schools were fanned by an old comrade of Theodore Roosevelt's, his field commander in the Spanish-American War, General Leonard Wood. Ending up at a desk job in Chicago, Wood carried on a minor crusade against foreignness in city schools during the winter of 1920 to gain publicity for his drive for the Republican presidential nomination.[6]

In 1908, Jane Addams, a Chicago friend of Dewey's, voiced concerns about the school as a melting pot. As committed as Dewey to the conception of the school as a social microcosm in which children learn through experience, she took issue with his view of the school relative to cultural difference. In an address to the National Education Association, she said:

> The public school too often separates the child from his parents and widens that old gulf between fathers and sons which is never so cruel and so wide as it is between the immigrants who come to this country and their children who have gone to the public school and feel that they have there learned it all. . . . At present the Italian child goes back to its Italian home more or less disturbed and distracted by the contrast between the school and the home. . . .
>
> We send young people to Europe to see Italy, but we do not utilize Italy when it lies about the schoolhouse. If the body of teachers in our great cities could take hold of the immigrant colonies; could bring out of them their handicrafts and occupations, their traditions, their folk songs and folk lore, the beautiful stories which every immigrant colony is ready to tell and translate; could get the children to bring these things into school as the material from which culture is made and the

---

[6] Herbert Mitgang, ed., *The Letters of Carl Sandburg* (New York: Harcourt, Brace, and World, 1968), p. 182.

material upon which culture is based, they would discover that by comparison that which they [the teacher] give them now is a poor meretricious and vulgar thing. Give these children a chance to utilize the historic and industrial material which they see about them and they will begin to have a sense of ease in America, a first consciouness of being at home. I believe if these people are welcomed upon the basis of the resources which they represent and the contributions which they bring, it may come to pass that these schools which deal with immigrants will find that they have a wealth of cultural and industrial material which will make the schools in other neighborhoods positively envious.[7]

We haven't paid much attention to Jane Addams. On the contrary, we have taken Dewey's rather moderate view of the school's assimilative function and made it a sort of moral imperative. We ignore the fact that assimilation destroys differences. Moreover, continuance of the "melting pot" ideology leads to the type of homogeneity necessary to bureautechnocracy and contributes to the decline of *person*. The carry-over of the "melting pot" ideology—from a period when it *may* have been *partially* defensible to an era which already suffers too much homogenization—is misguided and even dangerous. It has already led to a situation in education wherein we cannot tolerate difference in language or even language styles, cultures, habits, thought patterns, behaviors, and personalities. For example, our talk about achievement in school *suggests* a concern with individuality. If we reward achievement per se, then by definition we appear to be thinking in terms of the individual. But we do not reward achievement as such; rather, we reward the achievement (largely teacher perceived) of certain character types with which the teacher can deal.

James Coleman's data, as presented in *The Adolescent So-*

[7] Jane Addams, "The Public School and the Immigrant Child," *Proceedings of the NEA* (1909): 99–102.

ciety, make this clear. He shows that those who are identified as achievers in our schools are not necessarily the most academically able; they are merely willing to word hard at an activity which some teachers label as good. The standardized tests of intelligence which we use in our schools have long been shown to be culturally biased; they fail to speak to the intellectual capacity or even academic achievement of children whose language styles, subcultural values, and life experiences do not correspond to those of the white middle class. Yet we continue to use such tests on a massive scale. And we use them to categorize children as "bright," "average," "slow," and the like for purposes of classroom instruction. However absurd, these categories stay with children throughout most, if not all, of their school experience.

The wide variety of individual potentialities which children and youth bring to the classroom cannot be handled by a school whose orientation is the "melting pot" ideology. As Jules Henry says:

> American children, being American, come to school on the first day with certain potentialities for experiencing success and failure, for enjoying the success of their mates or taking pleasure in their failure, for competitiveness, for cooperation, for driving to achieve or for coasting along, et cetera. But school cannot handle variety, for as an institution dealing with . . . [a melting pot ideology] it can manage only on the assumption of a homogeneous mass. Homogeneity is therefore accomplished by defining the children in a certain way and by handling all situations uniformly. In this way no child is directly coerced. It is simply that the child must react in terms of the institutional definition or he fails. The first two years of school are spent not so much in learning the rudiments of the three R's, as in learning definitions.[8]

[8] Jules Henry, *Culture against Man* (New York: Random House, 1963), p. 292.

If you are a lower-class white child tested out as "slow" on any one of the several typically used standardized tests of intelligence, your chances of escaping this category, which is placed upon you very early in schooling, are very slim. If you are black, speak a nonstandard English dialect, or are foreign born and non-English speaking, your chances of escape are even slimmer. In short, an educational system pervaded by a "melting pot" ideology cannot meet the needs of all the individuals it purports to serve. The dangerous consequences of the "melting pot" theory become more striking when we look at this ideology in the framework of self-esteem.

Self-esteem, as we have seen, is based on a conscious awareness of one's self (and others) as a unique *person* whose individuality serves as agent of one's destiny. Our educators glibly speak of the schools' emphasis on the expression of personality and individuality, those things which make up *person*. The student quickly learns, however, that the personality and individuality of which they speak are not his, but a personality built on certain uniformities with which the school can deal. The individual person must be repressed, and that which is expressed as person must fit the institutional definition. We seem to overlook the fact in education that "it is not man that seeks a self, but each man; I want to be a self, and you do, and we want to be different selves. We think of mankind as a species, the human genotype, only as the faceless skeleton on whose bones our individual differences are molded. We are not asking for a universal self, but for ourselves. I want to be a self, and you want to be another; we want ourselves to be distinguishable; neither of us wants to be a duplicate copy of the other."[9] Because we forget about this need or desire for individuality, self, or *person*, today's education "metamorphoses the child, giving it the kind of *Self* the school can manage, and then proceeds to minister to the

[9] Jacob Bronowski, *The Identity of Man* (Garden City, N.Y.: Natural History Press, 1965), p. 10.

Self it has made."[10] Empirical evidence is available to support the existence of this problem. Rosenthal and Jacobson have shown (in *Pygmalion in the Classroom*) that children who are expected by their teachers to "fail" intellectually do fail, in terms of the assessments of these teachers, while those who are expected to gain do show greater intellectual gains as reflected in the assessments given them by the teachers involved.

Given its "melting pot" ideology, the school's predisposition to demand self-renunciation cuts off two main sources of self-esteem. First, the student is compelled to renounce self, whereupon identity comes to be located in things or people outside of self. Second, respect for others is stifled because the student is quick to learn that students, like members of society at large, are not dealt with as unique persons.

The constraints and restrictions on youth that we have discussed up to this point are alienating (that is their function) for they are part of the school's major function: to socialize youth into the culture of the school and, hence, the culture of the larger society. And socialization itself is alienating. As Friedenberg has noted:

> Socialization may best be defined as the systematic extinction of alternatives, the reduction of the potentially unassimilable view or disruptive thought to the level of the literally *unthinkable*. Socialization also, of course, emphasizes a complementary function: indoctrination or, as we more frequently choose to call it, "transmitting our cultural heritage"; that is, communicating to the young what may be thought or must be thought; what alternatives society will allow and even encourage. Education, indeed, in a period of little conviction, seems to consist primarily in communicating just this information; it does not seek to convince but to indicate subtly but clearly which interpretations of reality will be tolerated. Both repression and indoctrination work toward the same end: increased social stability on terms set by those currently in power and con-

[10] Henry, *Culture against Man*, p. 292.

sistent with the moral tradition they endorse; at the cost of alienating us from those of our feelings and insights that might impede the process.[11]

The most important function served by any educational system is that of providing the *means* for individuals to achieve an identity consciousness which brings self-esteem. In advanced industrial society, our schools, permeated by the "melting pot" ideology, are providing the means for identity consciousness, but they lead to that type of identity, supported by the culture of the larger society, which results in the loss of self-esteem. With both our educational system and society demanding a renunciation of *person*, we are rapidly reaching the point where such renunciation is becoming a moral imperative: "When we insist on taking a personal stand and bucking the system, we feel not only anxious, but guilty as well."[12]

Our analysis of self-esteem as it relates to culture and education is a macrocosm of the blacks' experience in white America. The cultural milieu enshrouding the education of black students, whether it be in the segregated school in the rural South or the segregated urban ghetto school, has the most debilitating effect upon respect for others and respect for self. Our total educational system has consciously or unconsciously chosen to overlook the culture and history of the black man; we have brutally cut him off from this cultural identity. In addition, we have effectively limited his ability to take pride in, and establish self-esteem in, his own physical identity.

The Negro today is reacting to these conditions by demanding control over his own destiny. He wants a black communal culture in which the *person* comes to exist through control over vital spheres of his life—his political destiny, his economic in-

11 Edgar Friedenberg, "Current Patterns of Generational Conflict," *Journal of Social Issues* 25, no. 2, p. 30.
12 Edgar Friedenberg, *The Vanishing Adolescent* (Boston: Beacon, 1964), p. 54.

dependence, his educational development. These demands signal a significant change in the relationship between the black and white communities. At present, the blacks appear to be less "concerned with winning white help than with asserting black autonomy as an intermediate but indispensable step on the path to true racial equality. The Negro's goal has shifted away from integration to economic and cultural independence from the white majority. He wants to be black, and he intends to emancipate himself."[13]

The blacks' demands are arousing people to a new understanding: assimilation of differences can be damaging. Cultural pluralism is the basis of a healthy society, and assimilation is contradictory to pluralism. The school must somehow scale down its assimilative pressures.

There is a logical connection between the school's "melting pot" ideology and those educational beliefs and practices which are based upon the extension of scientific liberalism.

EDUCATION AND SCIENTIFIC LIBERALISM

American schools are not like European *technicums*. Yet the influence of science in education cannot be denied. It is evidenced by (1) widespread acceptance of psychological testing, (2) grouping on the basis of the observable and measurable, (3) emphasis upon grading and grades, (4) heavy spending in the sciences at the expense of the humanities, and (5) the increasing use of and reliance upon the so-called new media, the "hardware" of educational processes. In just these few widely practiced processes one can see the influence of science in education. Society's intellectual foundation, its cognitive underpinning, has become education's intellectual foundation. Moreover, we build into our educational processes and institutions certain devices or practices which serve to determine the efficacy and

[13] "What Can I Do?" *Time*, May 17, 1968, p. 37.

efficiency of this intellectual foundation. An example of such a device is the already mentioned process of standardized psychological testing. Molnar notes:

> We take it increasingly for granted that at the important checking points of all these institutions [family, business, school] mental-mechanical devices are set up to regulate social traffic and individual destiny. Psychological tests are administered in schools, business corporations, the army, and even in certain ecclesiastical orders. Whatever we think of these tests—and the overwhelming evidence shows that they are wretched but pretentious fumblings with an immeasurable reality—they restrict and mechanize responses, and perform a selection that excludes the free, the imaginative, the morally and socially rebellious.[14]

Resistance to such devices has been neutralized.

> Resistance cannot be offered to these devices because they themselves confess to their present imperfection. The answer is more science, more scientific method applied to social, moral and emotional affairs. But it is not science alone that is held responsible for working out the correct solutions . . . for science to cover all relationships, it needs the cooperation of the whole social body, for how else could a machine operate unless all its parts are subordinated to the central purpose. In this way cooperation with expertise becomes a civic duty and a moral good; the organizational principle is imposed with a missionary zeal and accepted with that immemorial submissiveness with which man has always bowed to authority, however irrational, oppressive, or idiotic.[15]

The influence of science is also felt more subtly in mere day-to-day classroom pedagogy. Kimball and McClellan remind us that

[14] Thomas Molnar, *The Decline of the Intellectual* (Cleveland: World Publishing, 1961), p. 216.

[15] Ibid., pp. 216–17.

no one can seriously doubt that the honorific sense of the "scientific" dominates all classroom instruction: "What *really* happened?" "How can you explain that?" "What will happen if we do this?" "How do you know?" "What's the importance of that?" These are the standard classes of questions in ordinary pedagogy . . . asked in the teaching process. Now imagine two answers given to any one of them, one answer beginning, "Scientifically speaking . . . ," and the second, "Of course its unscientific to say so, but . . ." Which of these carries more weight, inspires more respect and attention? Please note that the answer would be the same whether we are speaking of the first grade or the fourteenth, of physical education, physics, civics, Russian history, English literature, or driver training.[16]

It is generally agreed that the enormous popularity of the scientific mentality in American education can be traced to the seminal theories of John Dewey. The five phases of what he called "The Complete Act of Thought" represented not only the paradigm of how a scientist qua scientist thinks but how all critical and reflective thought proceeds. He was straightforward enough about this position, remarking that the scientific method is "the sole ultimate resource of mankind in every field whatever."[17] Thus the five steps of what later came to be known as the "instrumental logic" became the model toward which all educational effort should be directed.

Effective education is, above all else, the scientific method at work in every area of experience. Far from being limited to scientific laboratories, this method is equally applicable to personal and social life. It is more than a precise method, however—more than the exactitude with which personal and so-

---

[16] Solon T. Kimball and James E. McClellan, Jr., *Education and the New America* (New York: Random House, 1966), p. 172.

[17] John Dewey, *The Quest for Certainty* (New York: Menton, Balch, 1929), p. 252.

cial problems are solved. It is the very quality with which humanity should approach all pressing problems. . . .

Good schools built on such a theory are potentially . . . culture's greatest single agency for genuine progress. Through them, the people can learn slowly how to act experimentally and so how to overcome the obstacles that always arise in the path of their onward march. Through them, the liberal way of life becomes synonymous with the democratic way.[18]

The last sentence in this quotation suggests that scientific method is synonymous with the "democratic way of life." This may be true in essence. That is, scientific method signifies those processes dominated by an attitude which goes something like this: "let us first examine the facts, and draw only such conclusions as the facts warrant. If no conclusion is warranted but some conclusion is necessary—since life does not wait on certainty—then let us hold the conclusion tentative and revise it as new evidence is gathered."[19] Accordingly, scientific method in its essence demands a move away from the authority of superstition, myth, or the dogma of some authoritarian individual or agency.

However, as noted in Chapter Four, although scientific method as a dominating influence may lead to the elimination of "absolute dogma," it appears to be leading to an absolute way of getting at knowledge, and to the negation of knowledge reached through means other than scientific method. Dewey may not have envisaged this for society at large, and we are convinced that he did not see this happening in education. Dewey's impact upon American education has thus contributed to a situation wherein schooling practices support the extension of scientific liberalism and, in turn, accommodate the imperatives of bureautechnocracy.

[18] Theodore Brameld, *Philosophies of Education in Cultural Perspective* (New York: Holt, Rinehart and Winston, 1955), pp. 90–91.

[19] Allen Wheelis, *The Quest for Identity* (New York: W. W. Norton, 1958), p. 73.

We noted in Chapter Four that the extension of scientific methodology into areas outside the "pure" sciences has come to dominate American intellectual life and in so doing has served to depersonalize and "de-individualize" our social relationships. This unhappy development shows the tragic irony of Dewey's thought. Dewey stressed the need for individuality in all aspects of living, and he lamented the fact that in education we submerge the individual with our inordinate concern for standardized averages, classes, and aggregates. He noted that "in spite of all our talk about individuality and individualism, we have no habit of thinking in terms of distinctive, much less uniquely individualized qualities."[20] Yet, whereas Dewey talked and wrote about the need for individualism in school and elsewhere, his emphasis on scientific method logically and factually led him to a greater concern with the group.

Dewey's goal in educational reform (and other reform for that matter) was a better *society*; this separates him from some other pragmatists, such as Schiller, whose aim in reform was for the *individual*.[21] Dewey stressed the social features of knowledge and meaning. He "went further than any of his predecessors in reinterpreting philosophy in *social* terms and spelling out the social and educational implications of the pragmatic method."[22] His emphasis on scientific method, which by definition is a search for social consensus, leads to the submission of the individual. A close reading of Dewey's work reveals that his position is permeated by objectivism and behaviorism.[23] Some writers have compared Dewey with other pragmatists, and with the existentialist point of view. William Barret has noted:

[20] John Dewey, "Individuality, Mediocrity, and Conformity in Education," in Carl H. Gross et al., eds., *School and Society* (Boston: D. C. Heath, 1962), p. 288.

[21] Kenneth Winetrout, *F. C. S. Schiller and the Dimensions of Pragmatism* (Columbus: Ohio State University Press, 1967), p. 45.

[22] Charles Frankel, as quoted ibid.., p. 46.

[23] Stephen S. White, as discussed ibid., p. 39.

Pragmatism meant something more and different for James than it did for Charles Sanders Peirce or John Dewey. The contrast between James and Dewey, particularly, shed light on the precise point at which Pragmatism, in the strict sense, ends and Existentialism begins. . . . The image of man as an earthbound and timebound creature permeates Dewey's writing as it does that of the Existentialists—up to a point. Beyond that point he moves in a direction that is the very opposite of Existentialism. What Dewey never calls into question is the things he labels Intelligence, which in his last writings came to mean simply Scientific Method. Dewey places the human person securely within his biological and social context, but he never goes past this context into that deepest center of the human person where fear and trembling start. Any examination of inner experience—really inner experience—would have seemed to Dewey to take the philosopher too far away from nature in the direction of the theological.[24]

Dewey's refusal to inquire into the truly individual is a function of his concern with scientific method. It should not surprise, therefore, that an educational system and process which is influenced by Deweyan thinking will be one that emphasizes the methodology of science and creates a microcosm of the conditions of society at large. Dewey's kind of educational system stresses adjustment to the group, skill in group decision-making, sociability, and consensus; it rewards those who follow directions, who sit still, and who submit to the renunciation of self. In all these ways Dewey's educational system is our system.

We have been altogether too succesful in perpetuating the view that the American school is the assimilator of differences. It is no wonder that in a school dominated by the scientific ethos, and "whose historical function has been making Americans out of immigrant's children, students are likely to find that they can only win esteem by how they look and behave, not for what

[24] As quoted ibid., p. 42.

they are. The effect of this is a servere form of alienation; they lose faith in their right to an independent judgment of their own worth."[25]

Social institutions, like individuals, are concerned with survival and with adjustment to survival conditions which incur the least amount of pain. All this involves a process of selective adaptation, and education has responded to the bureautechnocratic environment by taking on those structural and functional devices which appear to insure pain-free survival in bureautechnocracy. The scientific ethos is one of these devices. Another is bureaucracy itself, to which we now turn.

EDUCATION AND BUREAUCRACY

Perhaps the most significant change taking place in education during the last half century has been the increasing bureaucratization of the schools. The increasingly complex school administrative hierarchies, for example, and their big-business operations have led to a bureaucratic system and process which closely resembles that of a government agency or huge industrial corporation. We do not have to look beyond some very simple statistics to get a feeling for what this may suggest. In 1930 there were about 130,000 school districts in this country. In 1960 there were only about 20,000.[26] Anyone who spends time studying the public school system cannot help but sense the manner in which the system has become institutionalized into huge centralized bureaucracies, heavily dependent upon standardization, uniformity, and specialization of tasks. We do not imply that bureaucracies are inherently evil, but in the case of our school system, bureaucratization has led to impersonality

---

[25] Friedenberg, *The Vanishing Adolescent*, pp. 65–66.
[26] Patricia Sexton, *The American School: A Sociological Analysis* (Englewood Cliffs, N.J.: Prentice-Hall, 1967), p. 72.

in the schools in both their relationship with those that make up the system as well as with the public at large.[27]

Education's "selective adaptation" to bureautechnocracy increasingly resembles what has happened to individuals. It is not a matter of the school adjusting to its cultural milieu, but a matter of mimesis: education as process and institution is imitating bureautechnocracy. Mimesis has been generated by belief that schools are "factories" and students "raw" materials that will become "finished" products. And so educational processes increasingly resemble assembly line operations in which a conveyor belt receives the raw materials at one end and, after some minor changes and additions, delivers the finished product at the other. Although this may be something of an exaggeration, it cannot be denied that the factory notion of the educative process has had significant impact upon what we now do in schools. Ellwood Cubberly, whose administrative theories have been held up as models by generations of school administrators, spoke of the schools as "factories in which the raw materials are to be shaped and fashioned into products to meet the various demands of life."[28] The industrial or "factory" conception of the school still prevails, although its spokesmen are more sophisticated and their references to this conception less abrasive. One "expert" on education recently argued for the conception in this way:

> Like all industries, education is directed to a kind of market. "Market" is here used in its broadest sense to indicate a system of exchange where goods or services are given, for a price, to their beneficiaries. The price paid need not always be a monetary matter. In the case of education, somehow money is obtained to pay for the service. . . .

[27] Harry S. Broudy, B. O. Smith, and Joe R. Burnett, *Democracy and Excellence in American Secondary Education* (Chicago: Rand McNally, 1964), pp. 25–26.

[28] Ellwood Cubberly, *Public School Administration* (Boston: Houghton Mifflin, 1916), pp. 337–38.

We begin, then, with the perspective of education as an industry . . . whose service product gets distributed in a system which is at least analogous to a market system.[29]

The reason most often cited for the growth of educational bureaucracy is that it finally provides the types of services and resources necessary for a teacher to do his job well. There is serious doubt, however, whether this end is being realized. On the contrary, teachers and students are increasingly feeling the pressures which the rigidity of bureaucratic systems impose. More specifically, they feel impotent relative to changing conditions in their schools and classrooms, and they are increasingly dismayed with the decision-making procedures of their school systems, procedures which are logical consequences of bureaucratic organization.

Decisions made by administrators of an organization determine the method and content of classroom instruction, the size of the class, the goals of the organization, the characteristics of the classroom teachers, the hierarchy of personnel, the stratification of the students, and the degree of school-community interaction. Decisions made at the top can even abolish the classroom and establish alternative patterns of organization. . . . Such decisions could conceivably abolish teachers, change their functions, or otherwise dramatically alter the mode of instruction.[30]

The factory-like conception of schooling takes on more importance as large corporations move into the educational "industry" on a profit or nonprofit basis to package and sell books, programs, TV offerings, language laboratories, consultation services, and training programs. Most important in terms of long-

[29] James A. Schellenberg, "The Class-Hour Economy," in Dorothy Westby-Gibson, ed., *Social Foundations of Education* (New York: The Free Press, 1967), pp. 236–37.
[30] Sexton, *The American School*, pp. 65–66.

range implications, they are increasingly involving themselves in basic educational research and evaluation. Thus bureaucratization efforts are likely to be spurred on by the increasing influence of business in the schools, and technology—both hardware and rationalized procedures for achieving predetermined ends—will become more and more visible in educational institutions, the prevailing rationale for the management of American schools. Educational questions are often subordinated to considerations of business and efficiency. Schoolmen are now seduced into accepting new devices, programs, and machinery which have not been given the necessary examination they require to determine their effect on the learning process and on boys and girls. For example, television has many valuable uses for the classroom. But given bureaucracy in the schools, we increasingly turn to TV teaching not to improve instruction but to handle larger and larger classes. Efficiency comes before learning in the school's administrative value scheme.

Philosophies which once claimed a dualism between intellect and person have largely been rejected in contemporary educational thought. Indeed, in our latter-day "enlightenment" we thought we had driven out of educational practice those pedagogical tactics which seemed to have been generated by these dualistic theories. In point of fact, however, practices widely accepted and increasingly commonplace portend an unexamined return to the tacit belief that the "person" and the "intellect" (however they may be defined) are two entirely discrete and distinct entities. Teaching machines, closed-circuit television, packaged programs, and all our vast educational technology appear to be geared to a disembodied intellect—not to person.

Harold Hodgkinson (in *Education, Interaction, and Social Change*) writes of observing a demonstration of closed-circuit television teaching in which an excellent TV teacher was giving a demonstration of sculpture techniques. One little girl in the classroom was clearly excited with the project as she followed the teacher in fashioning her own piece of sculpture. As the program neared its end, the child could no longer contain her enthusiasm and pride of accomplishment. She grasped her sculpture, ran to the television monitor and said, "How's this, Miss Jones?" Miss Jones (on tape) droned on while the little girl, her pride rebuffed, returned to her seat in tears. The child thought she was dealing with a person and took on a role she usually played with persons. She certainly learned otherwise. Schooling (in Hodgkinson's instance) was for intellect; person was to be repressed.

The fact that we have largely rejected person-intellect dualism, and the fact that the increasing pervasiveness of our vast educational technology may breed educational practices which operate from the rejected dualism, points to our failure to analyze the new media critically. As educators we have simply submitted to the demands of bureautechnocracy's representatives, its marketeers and propagandists. We seem to operate on the tacit assumption (perhaps it is a rationalization of our submission) that the new technology is "neutral" or normless. But, of course, we know better. The new technology transforms whatever is processed through it or, in McLuhan terms, the message necessarily conforms to the abilities and limitations of the media.

Education survives in a bureautechnocratic environment by imitating it, but imitation can be carried too far: education is becoming increasingly depersonalized. Our schools represent few *human* values. What they do represent is an institution trying, with apparent success, to adjust to a machine-like system. This adjustment, this "conscious or unconscious aping of the industrial process . . . based upon coordination of men, machines, and materials . . . can only subvert the educative process."[31]

[31] Kimball and McClellan, *Education and the New America*, p. 212.

PART TWO

A New Kind of Education

CHAPTER 7

Bureautechnocracy and the Trivialized Man

THE ARGUMENT THUS FAR

At this point let us take a moment for consolidation, summing up the main arguments so far developed, and sketching out where these arguments seem to be leading.

In the first six chapters, we have constructed the following line of thinking. There has developed in America, over the last couple of generations, what amounts to a new social culture carrying with it the emotional freight and the psychological oppressiveness of a religion. We call this bureautechnocracy (Chapter 1). It has arrived quietly, maybe not on the proverbial cat's feet, but in a manner sufficiently unobtrusive as to surprise and startle us by its seemingly sudden presence. Bureautechnocracy may be defined as the pattern of social organization in which a pyramidal hierarchy of operational control is linked with rationalized and standardized means for reaching predetermined ends, with the overall aim of achieving systematization, efficiency, and economy. As represented in our government agencies, our schools, our churches, the military establishment, indeed in almost every social institution, but most of all in our occupational structures in business and industry, bureautechnocracy is the Number One ecological fact of our lives. It is the environment in which we live.

This environment is working its effects on all of us (Chapter 2). As individuals, we are gradually being homogenized. Of course, men living in communities have always tended to think, dress, and behave in ways similar to each other; but, for the most part, they were unaware of their conformities. Now, however, we experience the homogenizing process while it occurs; we can feel, as we undergo it, the pressure to regulate our public behavior to stay within the limits of community expectations. Unlike our predecessors, *we are aware of our homogenizability*.

The bitter harvest of all this (Chapter 3) is the growing sensation of being used by the system. We have become, whether we like it or not, instruments of the social order. Our wants are played upon and manipulated. Indeed, most of our needs are artificially created for us, and we easily succumb to the sirens of the market place. The system uses us in our work. We are carefully trained for our jobs, but when we perform them, our skills and functions—rather than our personal characteristics—become the defining qualities of our presence in the world; we are known as typists or shoe manufacturers. And finally we know: as both consumers and producers, we are replaceable. The system qua system needs people, but it does not absolutely *need me*. Not only are we alienated and isolated from each other, but indeed from ourselves. Our self-esteem is wounded; our quest for personal identity lashes out incoherently for symbolic supports in stainless steel things and "pay later" experiences.

But the trouble is deeper than that (Chapter 4). For the ideology of bureautechnocracy which has produced all this is cannibal. It eats its own children. It gobbles up and digests—the cliche is "co-opts"—whatever it generates, friend or foe. Any countermovement, any dissent, any disenchantment is somehow institutionalized, worked into the daily agenda as "part of the system," and eventually absorbed into the scheme of things. Protest and dissent are thus neutralized, defused, as we say of tomcats, "altered." What we have inadvertently created is an ideology of scientific liberalism, a social doctrine which has built into itself its own counterinsurgency mechanisms. It is immune to basic change, even while it allows superficial change to get the headlines and become advertisements for itself. It is an ideology in the classic sense of being quasi-religious in character, beyond mortal criticism. Finally, it is a liberalism which is, irony of ironies, anti-human—so in love with science and rationalism that it cannot recognize the simple human fact that some things about the world cannot be known through science and reason.

Nevertheless, the juggernaut of science rolls on. The scientists are determined to prove, as Dewey had prophesied, that the method of science can be extended to social, political, and moral affairs (Chapter 5). Man can be known, they insist, by studying his experience in the same way that we study a frog or a star—that is, by assuming that all phenomena somehow hang together in a system of cause and effect and mutual interrelatedness. Moreover, the rules of the knowledge game hold that only publicly verifiable assertions are admissible; all else is conjecture, opinion, myth, feeling, nonsense—in any case, not knowledge. What can be known about man is only that which can be known of an object, itself a system, which is behaving in a larger phenomenal system. Man as individual is, because unknowable, written off as not worth knowing.

This logic, if you want to call it that, has turned the public school in America into the perpetuator of the scientific bureautechnocratic system (Chapter 6). For over a century, the school has been admired as the one institution in American life deliberately designed as a human melting pot. And it has succeeded only too well, for it has snuffed out the sense of identity and self-esteem of countless millions who, through their allegedly egalitarian schooling, were taught to repudiate their own loyalties and feelings in the name of being "Americanized" into fit subjects for a bureautechnocratic state.

THE NEW CONSERVATISM

A few items in this catalogue of ideas need singling out for special attention. The first is the notion of a new conservatism which has taken hold of the American mind, a mentality of satisfied certainty about the basic wisdom of the American way.[1] Of course, we are all disenchanted with how things are going—violence in the streets, hatred in our communities, slaughter in southeast Asia. But we view these as surface aberrations of a system which is basically just and right. The naïveté and superficiality of our typically American response to trouble leads us to think that the corrective for the ills of our time is simply a more intense application of our general ideology of scientific liberalism: more study of the causes of violence, more control of the military-industrial complex, more organizational effort against intolerance, against poverty, against injustice. In short, the answer is more bureautechnocracy.

[1] An amusing lesson in political science is unfolding before our eyes. The old conservatives wanted to hold on to a set of transsocial values: hard work, saving for a rainy day, personal freedom, economic self-interest. The scientific liberals wanted to reexamine these values in light of social consequences, that is, apply the method of science to determine their social adequacy. But now, the liberals have grown conservative about the method; they want to hold on to it at all costs. Thus, the scientific liberals are now learning what the old conservatives have been trying to tell them for a hundred years: there is need for some sort of stability, an allegiance to some transsocial principle. The liberals have found it in science. Moreover, the liberals are quietly accepting another old conservative insight—there is need for an elite to make sure that the method of science is used correctly and protected from Philistine demands for harsh, unthinking "solutions" to social problems.

Now the New Left, rejecting both stability and elitism but adopting a little from each ethic—hatred of government from the conservatives, concern for the weak from the liberals—is bugging both right and left with its iconoclasm and demand for change and reform.

But sooner or later we must awaken to the possibility that the basic trouble may lie in the bureautechnocratic ideology itself and that a new ideology is called for. Ideology is moral attitude, an attitude toward what men ultimately want from their existence. This attitude is influenced, of course, by the kind of life a people builds for itself, its working ways, its institutional arrangements, its manner of getting things done. But, in the end, this attitude is a final term in the equation representing a theory of life. And it is a theory of life which tells us the most about ourselves and about the human enterprise.

The great danger of addressing oneself to the problem of a theory of life is precisely the danger of having to change one's mind about some very old cherished beliefs, most especially the beliefs dealing with the good and the bad in the world. And this is an undertaking to which enormous resistances have been built up. The surprise is not that these resistances develop; we know that. The surprise is that they should develop so readily and persist so vigorously in the American social climate. We have always prided ourselves on our flexibility and adaptability as a people. We have made a religion of change and elevated the concept of progress into an absolute moral good. But we are now embarrassed to learn that the social instrument we have developed for the orchestration of change—bureautechnocracy —is now itself above change, immune to criticism and firmly entrenched in the American mind as the only way to manage modern life. The complaint used to be that we were too materialistic, too obsessed with the plaything of technology to be capable of true culture. A more accurate complaint now would be that we are finding ourselves in the strange role of the new conservatives in a world of upheaval and resolution.

Perhaps we have reached a new epoch. A future history may be written about us. The latter nineteenth century will be billed as the coming of age of science and technology; we turned science to the business of making a living, built our industrial machine, and began cranking the stuff out. The first half of the twentieth century, with its wars, New Deals, Fair Deals, and social upheavals domestic and international, will be billed as the age of social science and institutionalized adjustment; we turned science to the business of human organization and behavioral management and succeeded in technologizing and bureaucratizing social behavior. But what will the history book say then? Reading the record from this close, we wonder if it will say that as we rationalized our physical environment and went on to rationalize our social environment, all in the name of science, we gradually lost interest in the whole sphere of human value, in the ultimate human question of how we *ought* to live. The book might say that, in the bureautechnocratic shuffle, men began to lose some of their humanness; they grew resistant to the difficult task of thinking about life, content to go on believing in the sacredness of science as applied to both things and men and willing to accept a system which indeed turns men *into* things as the necessary order of the human world.

Hopefully the history will say no such thing. It will say instead that, in the latter half of the twentieth century, men turned thoughtfully to the exciting business of human values. Having mastered nature and worked out at least partially effective social systems, they turned finally to the moral dimension of life and the business of learning how to live well. They began to assess their situation—the condition of existing amidst things *and people*— and to find there a newly realized excitement of being *individuals* intent on making themselves human again. To do this they found it necessary to advance to a new theory of life and learning, a new idea of what it takes to be a man.

THE EMERGENCE OF "META-BUREAUTECHNOCRACY"

We may not be ready for this new thrust forward. We seem to be—for the moment at least—still entangled in the second phase, the social epoch. We are trapped in organization; our feet are stuck in systems and system-driven groups. Of course, it is obvious that a modern society requires group design—in government, in corporate enterprise, in education and the arts. Research and invention now come from teams, planning and management are almost by definition plural in character, and culture and learning appear to be accessible only through large institutional structures and collective arrangements. Even the Great Books people found they had to market their Rational Humanism in groups![2] It is unlikely, therefore, that what we have produced so far in all of these sectors of modern life could have been possible without the instrument of collective effort.

But the dependence upon collectivities continues to evolve. It has gone on to a more advanced stage, a stage we may call "acute Parkinsonianism." Not only have bureaucracies multiplied, expanding their functions to absorb the unutilized labor of the people they have already hired, and then hiring more to carry on the new functions as these functions are expanded in order to absorb the unused man-hours of the new group—not only this, but bureaucracies now appear to be exhibiting a more sophisticated tendency, namely, creating the need for whole new "second-generation" bureaucracies.

Labor unions are themselves, in their home offices, having labor troubles. They are now bargaining with the labor unions representing their own employees. Some of these negotiations are not a little amusing, and the presumption is that the parent unions are beginning to see themselves as employers, as "management," a new irony not lost on the people sitting on either side of this curious conference table. Government is now getting so large and complex that there must be a special agency within it to govern the intramural aspects of its work—that is, to pro-

---

[2] Indeed, a movement has developed to repudiate groups, but the movement itself has had to organize! The American Humanist Association runs a regular ad in the *Saturday Review* with the plea: "We need members who are reluctant to join organizations."

vide a government of the government. At the federal level, this agency is called the General Services Administration (GSA), a unit customarily referred to as the "housekeeping" branch—a metaphor as accurate as any to show the direction in which things are going. In educational institutions, the cadres of "administrators" have finally managed to earn the suspicion and contempt which teaching faculties have often unthinkingly heaped upon them; they have Parkinsonized their functions so successfully that they now require their own internal administrators, "deans of administration," as they are called, who sit not atop but somewhere within the hierarchy of the various schools and faculties. In other words, the deans themselves now have their own dean who, with his own staff of scribes, bookkeepers, and watchdogs, "keeps house" in the internal running work of a modern university.

There is an even more advanced stage of the organizational tendency, a phenomenon which, while hard to explain and a little frightening, is probably inevitable. We shall call it "metabureautechnocracy," that is, organizations themselves now banding together into organizations. The associations of various kinds of intellectuals band together to call themselves the American Council of Learned Societies. Trade associations, business groups, and chambers of commerce get together to form such bodies as the Joint Council on Economic Education. Accrediting associations, themselves organizations of organizations (i.e., schools and colleges), have joined to form the National Council on Accreditation. There is even one case we know of in which an outfit called the Associated Organizations for Teacher Education has, as one of its members, an organization called the American Association of Colleges for Teacher Education which, in turn, includes a number of large universities which, finally, are made up of still smaller organizations, namely colleges (some of which train teachers)—in other words, *four* layers of organizations before you get to individuals!

It is not altogether idle to speculate on the causes of this lengthening series of Chinese boxes. We suspect that at the bottom of the whole movement lies a fact which is the direct outgrowth of a highly technologized and bureaucratized society: *there is not enough work for everybody*. We have certainly seen in agriculture the gradual shrinkage of that percentage of our population required to produce all the food and fiber we can comfortably use up and wear out: a couple of centuries ago it was close to 90 percent, today it is in the vicinity of seven percent and (according to census information) still dropping. It is no secret, in Washington or anywhere else, that the basic cause of agricultural surpluses is the surplus of farmers in our economy.

With the advance of the mechanized production line and, now, the onrush of automated manufacturing processes, the economy has seen a gradual reduction also in the number of man-hours required to run the industrial complex. Even with the instrument of research, by which we have institutionalized invention and discovery, we have been unable to create new products and (with advertising) the artificial need for them fast enough to absorb the surplus labor potential of the productive work force. Unemployment is now a chronic threat.

The result has been the gradual turning of the labor force to service occupations[3] wherein individuals simply do something for somebody else, the "taking in of each other's washing" on a vast, continental scale. Inevitably, as the services expand and become more complex and intricate—say, the Social Security system in Washington or guidance and testing offices in today's schools—the need for organization increases. And since there is not enough work for all in direct production or direct service, our society can tolerate the build-up of the very specialized service of *organizing organization itself*. This is done practically by organizing organizations into ever larger entities with ever larger scope. There is apparently no end to the increasing re-

[3] During the 1950's, the United States became the first country to employ more people in service occupations than in production occupations.

lease of surplus labor from production industries and, now, even from the service occupations (for instance, the use of dictating machines and, more recently, automatic file systems and electronic accounting devices). It is because of this that the tendency to organize organizations as such is inevitably destined to expand.

We needn't wring our hands over this, however. There is nothing intrinsically wrong with the creation of increasingly trivial things for people to do. The hazard lies in the effect of this trivialization upon the individuals involved. This effect, we believe, is not just an idle by-product of organization society; rather, it is a new fact of civilized life destined to work its pressure on the remolding of human attitudes.

For one thing, there is a developing sense of aimlessness among those for whom work is largely the shuffling of papers and the keeping of records. There was a time, earlier in our industrial history, when the grinding demands of the factory assembly line were thought to be turning laborers into slaves to their machines, inevitably dehumanizing them into vacant, mindless animals turning cranks and pulling levers. There was a real danger, we believed, that the psychological impoverishment of eight hours of bolt-tightening might bring men to their spiritual knees, making them unfit for the enjoyment of whatever new leisure this system might provide. It is possible that some of this impoverishment has occurred; but in retrospect the laborer appears to have survived this epoch in industrial development, an epoch we expect soon to pass with the increasingly automated factory. He has survived production-line ennui because, while he knew himself to be only a cog in a large, impersonal, corporate machine, he still could touch the thing he was helping to make—an automobile, a toaster, a radio—and sense somehow the importance, slim as it was, of his participation in its creation. Moreover, whatever psychological impoverishment he suffered was made up for by a very sweet pay envelope.

But the ennui of organization paper work may be of a different order of magnitude. It is true that paper work by definition deals with symbols, that is, words and numbers; and it should be, therefore, intrinsically more interesting and satisfying than production-line work. Also, it is more likely to deal with people than with things, and hence, be more personally rewarding. But the fact of the matter is that it is fundamentally less important and lower paying. Where the bolt-tightener had a relatively clear notion that he was needed, that he had to show up for work to tighten the bolts, the paper shuffler and organization man carries around an uneasy awareness of his expendability. It is a not altogether facetious observation that the troops of bureau-technocracy are reluctant to take long vacations lest the triviality of their functions become known. Having neither a concrete "product" or vital "service" to identify with, their only attach-ment is to the organization as such, and their remoteness from the actual marketplace of goods and services is reflected in neatly embossed but piddling paychecks.

In the face of this, organization people have tended to create their own work—as Parkinson has told us—and to discover new functions within the organization which, they hope, will be rec-ognized as duties which the organization can less afford to do without than the originally assigned functions. It is the rare fac-tory worker who has been motivated in this direction.

THE TRIVIALIZED MAN

In any event, the inroads of trivialism upon the human spirit cannot be underestimated. Even if an individual is secure in his job and can afford the psychological luxury of long vaca-tions, and even if he has carved out what to him is an important corpus of work, there lingers the suspicion whispering within him that his labors day after day are not absolutely needed. He needs his paycheck much more than his organization needs his services. He shows up for work, especially on paydays, but his organization can tolerate ever lengthening coffee breaks and lunch hours because the work, if you want to call it that, does not really have to be done. Work used to be thought of as potentially ennobling, by Marx and others, in giving the individual a grip on his world and an opportunity to put his stamp on it; or, in contrast, it was a necessary nuisance left over from the Puritan days of "scarcity" economics. Nowadays, however, it appears that work is neither of these, but rather a pleasant social interlude to fill the hours prior to cocktail, prime ribs, and the evening's television.

To characterize work as a social interlude suggests a second, and perhaps more dehumanizing, element of organization life: the immersion of the individual in group culture. We needn't re-run here the by now old movies of Riesman, Whyte, Lynes, and Packard. Rather, we need to pick up from them and run the story a little further by saying that immersion in the "culture of others" not only compromises the autonomy of the individual but also cuts down and subtracts from that area of the world he may call his own—namely, the sense he has of his own self-identity. To breathe heavily of the atmosphere of "others" is to risk being vaporized as a center of moral action; and it is this process of vaporization which is now in a dangerously advanced stage of development in American life.

The risk in taking the cue from others in shaping our own experience is hazard enough, even though it would seem to follow naturally from the kind of social life we have worked out for ourselves. But a deeper risk, potentially more damaging, is not recognizing that we are doing the "taking" as *active* moral agents in the moral encounter. To take the cue from others is *to take*, and *to take* is an active verb meaning *to choose* a certain kind of living. And *to choose* ultimately carries moral implications which we are obliged to consider if a new theory of life is to be made possible.

The significance for our argument is this: people who have built organization life up around them show symptoms of not being completely awake in the moral encounter where choosing is going on. Organization man is, either by definition or derivation, *gregarious* man. He enjoys being with and among people, and that means he enjoys the human interplay of stimulus and response in and for itself. So thoroughly has he been embraced by organization life that he has come to feel that gregariousness itself is a kind of moral necessity, a requisite means to the finding of meaning in his existence. He takes gregariousness for granted; it is a kind of "given" in his world, like trees and governments. And he comes to the view that the world is built along lines in which good mixing, social adjustment, and shared interests are the primary counters in the human enterprise.

In actual fact, gregariousness is not a "given" so much as a "taken," something actively opted for, pulled out of the universe of possibilities and adopted for one's life. To find oneself living the gregarious life is to find oneself having *chosen* it as a moral dimension of human experience. We live what we choose man to be. The awareness of this fact is not, to permit an understatement for our times, the general property of those we call organization people.

In sum, modern bureautechnocratic man has had his work taken away from him and his fellow citizens clumped around him. His sense of life has been diverted from what he does to whom he does it with. It is in this specific sense that we can speak of his having achieved the "trivial state." For in leaving his work and turning to other people—to feel some sort of meaning in his life and achieve some sort of "identity"—he settles for a universe of possibilities which is necessarily restricted. His pool of options is reduced in scope because he has decided to listen only to a narrow segment of option-makers—that is, the other people with whom he comes in contact daily. Like the newspaper reporters who predicted the election of Thomas Dewey in 1948 by interviewing each other, modern bureautechnocratic man consults only the expectations of those in his own social class, business group, or social crowd to decide what to make of his life. He knows what they are advising him to do and how they think he should live his life, but he does not realize that he is taking their advice. He knows what he is choosing, but he is not aware *that* he is choosing.

It is *the awareness of choosing* as such which is being vaporized away. As the awareness fades and our behavior becomes more the conditioned reflex to a bureautechnocratic social machine, our having been trivialized is only dully sensed in the dimmer regions of our sensibilities. It is the awakening of these sensibilities which constitute the summary call of the modern educator.

WHAT NEEDS DOING

We come then to the final argument of this book. What, if anything, can the professional educator do to reclaim the lost chances of an earlier epoch? If individualism has been fought for and lost—from Rousseau and Thoreau, through James and Dewey, to Skinner and McLuhan—what new strategies can be devised to carry the attack once more to some sort of victory, however partial it may be? What, in short, can today's educator do to awaken the sense of awareness of individual choosing? Is there a new schooling, a new mode of teaching and learning, which may arouse the sensibilities of the young—and the old, too, for that matter—to the possibilities for self-direction and idiosyncratic decision-making?

We think there is, and we attempt in the following two chapters to sketch out the general outlines of such a pedagogical theory. Chapter Eight offers what amounts to a new epistemology, a new way of looking at knowledge. It goes by a number of names —personal knowledge, the affective domain, intersubjectivity, private awareness. But, whatever the label, it is a zone of knowing and understanding which has systematically been depreciated in a scientized age. Its weakened condition is the number one symptom of the malaise of bureautechnocratic man.

With this epistemology in place, we then limn the outline of a new education. Chapter Nine offers an analysis of some of the main conceptual members of such a pedagogy. If a new zone of human understanding, crowded out and cheapened by a technologized and bureaucratized age, is in need of clearer identification, how may the educator fan the faint flames of such understanding in young people as they mature to make a life of their own? Specifically, how do teachers teach and learners learn in this new mode?

We turn to these questions now.

CHAPTER 8

Human Knowing

SCIENCE'S LIMITS

Philosophers and educators have always held one passionate interest in common: what is knowledge, and how do we come to know it? Professionally, this interest goes by the name of epistemology, the study of knowledge and the act of knowing. Philosophers are perhaps more interested in knowledge itself, but they realize that what knowledge is depends to a great extent, if not absolutely, on how one attains it; a truth which is reached through private intuition is a different beast from a truth reached through sense perception. An educator, on the other hand, focuses on the latter question: how do human beings come to know things? But he soon realizes that that can be answered only when we decide what is worth knowing, what the child should be asked to learn. So the two concerns are indissolubly linked.

Over the centuries, both philosophers and educators have had to shift their search for knowledge more and more to the empirical world. Whereas Plato and the Greeks looked for truth in some ultimate realm beyond the world, and medieval theologians thought they might find it in the mind of God, modern thinkers have pretty much given up on these far-out expeditions and explored the possibilities for knowledge closer to home, in the ordinary experience of mortal human beings.

But "the ordinary experience of mortal human beings" turns out to be not so ordinary. It is a vast, complex sphere of awareness in which a great many notions can pass for knowledge, even though on closer inspection their credentials seem very shaky. (Professional golfer Bert Yancey says that the brass "voodoo bracelet" on his right wrist eases the pain in his elbow when he swings by absorbing acids in his body. Is Yancey's "truth" a piece of knowledge, or is it a piece of Yancey's imagination?) The task of today's epistemologist is to sort out the many varieties of knowledge-producing experiences to see which of them men can put the most trust in.

Without any question, "the champ" in this regard is science. As a way of knowing, it does yield a dependable and reliable form of knowledge; it allows us to make predictions and exercise control. Of course, as we all know, this kind of knowledge often turns out to be wrong; but modern men have gotten used to that. Indeed, they rather expect that what science knows about the world at any given moment is bound to be corrected and improved upon by the next generation of scientists. We should notice, however, that when a scientific proposition turns out to be incorrect it does not throw the whole human race into a despondent fit, as is the case when a metaphysical or theological proposition is shown to be incorrect. Since science deals with smaller particles of the phenomenal world than metaphysics or theology, its mistakes are less traumatic. But that is precisely because its claims to large, cosmic truth are also much more modest. Science promises less, and it delivers less. Both its pretentions and its products are not very grand. Modern men have come to find a certain measure of honest satisfaction in this less megalomanic epistemology.

However, the irony of our day is that science has surreptitious-

ly developed its own megalomania. It has achieved such stupefying victories in the physical environment that its practitioners
now consider themselves qualified to take over social and behavioral phenomena, and even morals and ethics. But these
territories are not so easily invaded; when they are, we witness
a despoliation of the landscape so severe as to make us wonder
about the legitimacy of the invader.

By way of example, we may review some earlier observations
in this volume. In Chapter Four, we have documented the thesis
that science, when applied to human behavior, shows us how to
predict the corporate behavior of a businessman, how to create
needs in people which they do not have and do not want, how to
arrange conditions in which people will lie to one another, how
to change people's minds, how to alter a person's view of himself
and demolish his ego.

Following this, we have shown how the whole mentality of
science gets converted into an ideology now beyond criticism.
Scientific liberalism is the new dogma. Anything that can be
known through science, we are told, *should* be known. And it
doesn't matter whether you have to turn human beings into
things in order to discover it; if it is scientific, it not only should
be, but *must* be, known.

We have seen also that scientific liberalism is now the main
intellectual support for bureautechnocracy. It has become the
instrument for depersonalizing the entire knowing process.
Scientific liberalism has bureaucratized the act of inquiry so
that today large armies of technicians, research engineers, statis-
ticians, computer programmers, behavioral psychologists, ur-
banologists, and graduate assistants (epistemological spear-
carriers!) move their expertise and their apparatus into almost
any area of investigation with impunity, almost as if it would be
rude and disrespectful of the ideology to deny them access to
what they want to find out. In short, knowing itself has become
a bureautechnocratic industry in its own right.

SCIENCE AS A COUNTERHUMANISM

But now are there other, deeper troubles with science? Could science as an epistemology possibly break out of its narrow bed and become human? We believe the answer must be "No." And we build our case on three final charges which we now specify: (1) science, by definition, is incapable of studying the individual; (2) science, by definition, converts the experienced world into a nonhuman form; (3) science brutalizes man. We take these up in order.

As a mode of knowing, science is what the technical philosopher refers to as "reductionistic." That is, science attempts to reduce to the fewest possible propositions the number of things that can be said about the world. In our common talk, we speak of this as "generalization": the effort to gather up several phenomena under one general idea. We have become familiar with this in, say, biology, in which discipline the varieties of flora and fauna, representing billions of individual organisms, are classified and described by botanical and physiological principles which enable us to order and systematize our understanding of the world of living things. We are not particularly interested in a solitary nasturtium or bumblebee; rather, we are hopeful of comprehending how *all* nasturtiums and *all* bumblebees function. This kind of knowledge is not only a delight in itself, but it enables us to *predict* and *control* our experience with these organisms; it helps us *use* nasturtiums and bumblebees by turning their presence in the world to our own account—as decorations for our enjoyment or as pollinators of our cherry trees.

When science turns to the study of man, it necessarily must remain true to its own logic. It cannot deal with individual entities in their uniqueness; it must deal instead with classes of beings which are to be understood entirely in terms of shared properties.

Consider by way of illustration the so-called science of psychology. Either the would-be scientist of human behavior follows the lead of the experimental psychologist who succeeds in making reasonably accurate generalizations but only by limiting his study to the most trivial aspects of human behavior; or else he follows the lead of the clinical psychologist who deals with more important human problems but only by introducing such vague categories that we do not even know how to go about determining the accuracy of his generalizations.[1]

Psychologists themselves have become more and more sensitive to this limitation to their work. Some have attempted a new departure in psychological inquiry, namely, a search for the self or the person somewhere "within" the behaving subject. Among the most earnest and sincere in this effort is Carl Rogers, certainly one of the major figures in American psychology in the twentieth century. In a widely studied essay, "Toward a Science of the Person," he separates three kinds of knowing: subjective, objective, and interpersonal or phenomenological. In discussing objective knowing as the paradigm of science he says:

Since [this mode] deals only with observable objects, the elements of any problem studied by such an approach must be treated only as publicly observable objects. Thus if I wish to study the effect upon myself of a fever-inducing drug, I observe myself as an object. . . . Objectivity can only be concerned with objects, whether these are animate or inanimate. Conversely, this way of knowing transforms everything it studies into an object, or perceives it only in its object aspects.[2]

But the pathos of Rogers's good intentions is the occasion for heartbreak six pages later when he reveals that he himself is the

[1] Robert Olson, "Science and Existentialism," address delivered at Rutgers University, October 17, 1963.
[2] Carl Rogers, "Toward a Science of the Person," in T. W. Wann, ed., *Behaviorism and Phenomenology* (Chicago: University of Chicago Press, 1964), p. 113.

captive of the objective, scientific imperium. He ruins whatever credibility he had built up by saying, "[The phenomenological-existential trend in psychology] will throw open the whole range of human experiencing to scientific study. It will explore the private worlds of inner personal meanings in an effort to discover lawful and orderly relationships there."[3] So, sad to say, we are going to objectify inner personal meanings, single them out for analysis, and determine the laws which govern their appearance. That is, we are going to apply the "reductionist" logic of objective science to the most individual and personal of phenomena; Rogers actually cites studies in which these investigations have begun. He sums up:

> The lessons which I only very slowly assimilated from this experience were these: (1) It is possible to measure phenomenological variables with a reliability which compares with the reliability of measuring complex behavioral variables. (2) If our aim is to discover variables which have potency, are predictive, and show significant functional relationship with important externally observable events, then well-selected phenomenological variables may be even more likely than behavioral variables to exhibit such potency. The inner world of the individual appears to have more significant influence upon his behavior than does the external environmental stimulus.[4]

As a living exhibit of how a scientist can get sucked in to his own predispositions, Rogers utters this puzzling final word:

> This phenomenological-existential movement . . . represents a new philosophical emphasis. Here is the voice of subjective man speaking up loudly for himself. Man has long felt himself to be but a puppet in life—molded by economic forces, by unconscious forces, by environmental forces. He has been

[3] Ibid., p. 119.
[4] Ibid., p. 125.

enslaved by persons, by institutions, by the theories of psychological science. But he is firmly setting forth a new declaration of independence. He is discarding the alibis of *un*freedom. He is *choosing* himself, endeavoring, in a most difficult and often tragic world, to *become* himself—not a puppet, not a slave, not a machine, but his own unique individual self. The view I have been describing in psychology has room for this philosophy of man.[5]

Yet Rogers himself, just a few pages earlier, has inadvertently admitted that man is *not* unique—his inner meanings can be plotted on a graph in order to reveal laws and orderly relations of the inner life!

We do not expect a scholar of Rogers's credentials to contradict himself so ingenuously. He should be able to realize that man cannot choose himself so long as his "inner world" becomes a bag of "phenomenological variables" which are "predictive" of his experience. How can a man be free if his future experience can be predicted?

We offer Rogers as the tragic example of trying to have it both ways, of trying to have science and the free person in one and the same breath. But it cannot be done, and that is because science, simply because it *is* science, cannot know the unique person. There is no such thing as a "science of the person." It is a contradiction in terms.

We turn now to the second of our charges against science—namely, that it converts the experienced world into a nonhuman form. Some years ago, Abraham Kaplan, in a book entitled *The Conduct of Inquiry*, remarked that the scientific method has become a fascination for modern man, partly because we have become more enchanted by *how* things are done than *what* things are done, more beguiled by *process* than *product*.[6] So advanced is this syndrome that we push the "process" mold down

---

[5] Ibid., p. 130.
[6] See John A. Kouwenhoven, "What's American about America?" *Harper's*, July, 1956, pp. 25–33.

upon all that we do so as to make experience take on the con-
tours of our familiar ways of dealing with it. Kaplan says:

> It comes as no particular surprise to discover that a scien-
> tist formulates problems in a way which requires for their
> solution just those techniques in which he himself is especially
> skilled.
>   . . . [In the scientific community] there is . . . at work a
> very human trait of individual scientists. I call it *the law of the
> instrument*, and it may be formulated as follows: Give a small
> boy a hammer, and he will find that everything he encounters
> needs pounding.[7]

So it is with our science. Give man science, and everything in
his experience takes on significance only if it can be made to
yield to science.

Psychology, as a case in point, used to be literally the study
of "the psyche." But since the psyche could not be studied by
scientific measures, psychology gradually had to be converted
into the study of "behavior." Behavior is something you can
see; you can measure it, plot it on graph paper, run statistics on
it, punch holes in IBM cards for it, and make a computer "eat
it." Psychology has thus been "scientized." And even the nostal-
gia of Rogers cannot rescue it.

Advertising, to take another, used to be the innocent effort to
make known to other people what you had to offer them. Now
it has become the industry of determining how much mileage
you can get out of other people's economic behavior. The adver-
tiser gradually becomes interested in the process for its own
sake. What shape bottle will sell the most Coke? What editorial
ambience will build the largest magazine circulation? What
combination of TV fun and nonsense will get the highest ratings?
No matter how good, just how much? What science touches it
quantifies, because that is the only way science knows how to

[7] Abraham Kaplan, *The Conduct of Inquiry* (San Francisco: Chandler,
1964), p. 28.

work. But the human world is built of *qualities*, and on these science is dumb.

We see, then, that science can "understand" the world only by converting it into a nonhuman sphere of phenomena: quantities, measurements, dial readings, group behavior, cause-and-effect linkages, and the chopping up of lived life into discrete and isolated variables. In such an atmosphere, much of the human spirit finds difficulty breathing.

Finally, science brutalizes. This is admittedly a serious charge to make, especially in light of all that science has done for us in medicine, hygiene, nutrition, sanitation. But these are the ironies which, so to speak, prove the rule. For medicine and public health are flamboyantly open and overt in their results; science works more stealthily and unobtrusively. It commands our attention so much as a method of knowing that we become insensitive to who gets hurt in the process.

Perhaps one of the more benign examples of this is in the classic work of Robert Rosenthal and Lenore Jacobson, *Pygmalion in the Classroom*.[8] This remarkable study was undertaken to attempt to show a very important truth about human beings— that "one person's expectation for another person's behavior can quite unwittingly become a more accurate prediction simply for its having been made." Specifically, the study was "addressed to the question of whether a teacher's expectation for her pupils' intellectual competence can come to serve as an educational self-fulfilling prophecy."[9]

Here is a perfectly legitimate and testable scientific hypothesis, capable of being verified or disproven through standard empirical means. But in order to set up the situation to extract the data, Rosenthal and Jacobson had to work a deception on more than fifty teachers. They "administered" a meaningless test, "The Harvard Test of Inflected Acquisition," to the chil-

---

[8] Robert Rosenthal and Lenore Jacobson, *Pygmalion in the Classroom* (New York: Holt, Rinehart and Winston, 1968).
[9] Ibid., p. vii.

dren; with the alleged "results" of this test they deceived the
teachers into believing that certain pupils in their rooms were
"late bloomers" about to make a significant spurt forward in
scholastic achievement. The hypothesis was confirmed: pupils
expected by their teachers to make forward spurts did so; other
pupils, equal in every way to the first group, but *expected not* to
make forward spurts, did not.

What price did we pay for this scientific finding? Two scientists, dedicated to the truth, told a lie, not just as a social nicety,
but *in the line of duty as scientists*. And nowhere in their report
do they express even the faintest remorse for this inhuman act.
Their passion for science has driven out their compassion for
their fellow man.

Or consider the work of Stanley Milgram. A Yale psychologist,
he learned his trade from one of the old masters in experimental
psychology, Solomon Asch. His technique is "to stage a play
with every line rehearsed, every prop carefully selected, and
everybody an actor except one person. That one person is the
subject of the experiment. The subject, of course, does not know
he is in a play. He thinks he is in real life. The value of this
technique is that the experimenter, as though he were God, can
change a prop here, vary a line there, and see how the subject
responds.[10]

A volunteer for an educational experiment is asked to be the
"teacher" while another "volunteer" (a member of the experimental team) assumes the role of "learner." The "learner," sitting in a separate room, is strapped with electrodes connected
(so the "teacher" is led to believe) to a switch in front of the
"teacher" which will send a shock of varying intensity through
the electrodes to the "learner" when a wrong answer is given.
Using word-matching schedules for "teaching materials," the
"teacher" voices the stem word through an intercom, and with
each successive wrong answer gives the "learner" a stronger

---

[10] Philip Mayer, "If Hitler Asked You to Electrocute a Stranger, Would
You?—Probably," *Esquire* 74, no. 2, p. 73.

jolt. If the "teacher" hesitates, no matter how far up the voltage scale he goes or how agonized the cries of pain from the other room, the experimenter insists that he continue. The object is to find the shock level at which you disobey the experimenter and refuse to pull the switch.

At the "Pygmalion" level of scientific dishonesty, Milgram has of course deceived in order to get a truth. Unlike Rosenthal and Jacobson, he ponders the morality of it, but has resolved the problem in his own favor, claiming that his unknowing subjects are free to leave at any time whereas the experiment's "man in the electrodes" is not. But more important, the truth he gets, through the big lie, shows how far we have been brutalized by science: "sixty-five percent of the subjects, twenty to fifty-year-old American males, everyday, ordinary people, like you and me, obediently kept pushing those levers in the belief that they were shocking the mild-mannered learner . . . all the way up to 450 volts."[11]

These experiments took place in the early 1960's. The results were far more startling than Milgram had anticipated, and ever since he has been trying to figure out what makes ordinary American citizens so obedient.

> The most obvious answer—that people are mean, nasty, brutish and sadistic—won't do. The subjects who gave the shocks to Mr. Wallace [the victim's pseudonym] to the end of the board did not enjoy it. They groaned, protested, fidgeted, argued, and in some cases, were seized by fits of nervous, agitated giggling.
>
> "They even try to get out of it," says Milgram, "but they are somehow engaged in something from which they cannot liberate themselves. They are locked into a structure, and [cannot] disengage themselves."[12]

That structure, we now know, is science. The subjects were obedient to the experimenter because they felt the obligation

[11] Ibid., p. 130.
[12] Ibid.

being imposed on them by the system. For most subjects, says Milgram, the act of giving Mr. Wallace his painful shock was necessary, even though unpleasant; besides, they were doing it on behalf of somebody else, and it was for science.[13] So, in this quiet, unobtrusive way, science has become the new imperium. Science for its own sake comes to outrank all other loyalties. Science has become the holy principle of our time. In its name, cruelty to another human being can be justified.

We close this catalogue of instances with a gross and probably undocumentable bit of phenomenological evidence, namely, the gradual change in our sensitivity regarding human life itself, occasioned we believe by the domination of the scientific mentality. The American imagination is uplifted by spectacular scientific achievements—satellites hanging in the sky, hearts transplanted from one man to another, rockets voyaging to the moon. But there is the same kind of awe expressed for the nuclear bomb. We see this wondrous and stupefying explosion. At first we are shaken, almost metaphysically moved, by the wordlessness of it. But then we regain our scientized pride. We preen. We say, "Man can make a sun. . . . How about that!" There is this awesome whisper of sophisticated disbelief, the voiceless, breath-catching question—what hath *man* wrought? And we are full of wonder. But we are proud of being able to make ourselves wonder. Oh yes, someone says, one hundred thousand human beings died at Hiroshima—brothers, sisters, sons, daughters, mothers, fathers. Yes, those are the statistics—one hundred thousand people—very hard to comprehend. What an explosion!

THE DEMON WITHIN

Where is the human in us? If science turns us away from ourselves, away from what we want our "human-being-ness" to be, then where do we look for the answer? Does the solution lie

13 Ibid., p. 132.

simply in less science? Will bureautechnocracy go away if we individually try to be less scientific in our daily routines? Or is a positive effort called for? Is there a zone of human existence which is calling out for exploration and development, a region of humanness which has been there all along but has been pressed out of our awareness for too long? We think there is. And we think that a deliberate expedition into that region will remind both philosophers and educators that their homework on man isn't done. In order to get a plot on the territory we wish to inspect, we turn to an analogue from an unlikely source, Aristotle.

In the *Politics*, Aristotle sought to articulate the best form of government. But in his search, he recognized that a prior understanding must be the nature of happiness. Happiness, however, is a fugitive notion, extremely difficult to surround and understand. The Greeks thought they had it:

> The Greek word which is translated "happiness" is *eudaimonia*. Another standard rendition is "prosperity." The adjective from the same roots refers to a condition brought about by a good (*eu*) genius or demon (*daimon*). Thus, to the extent that we allow fortune to be personified and to be responsible for all that "happens" (as in our word "happiness"), "good fortune" or "happiness" will serve as fair literary translations. But these are not acceptable philosophically, precisely because they are associated with the idea of an *external* minor deity, a demon, whose favor is gained or received. It is the *externality* of the genius or demon which the main tradition of Greek philosophy rejects.[14]

Instead, said Aristotle, the essence of happiness is to be found in some quality of man which is indigenous to him, which he carries around inside him all the time. Thus a man's condition is not governed by what happens *to* him, but by what is happen-

[14] Robert S. Brumbaugh and Nathaniel M. Lawrence, *Philosophers on Education* (Boston: Houghton Mifflin, 1963), p. 52.

ing *within* him. Even modern man has consistently failed to see this. We believe that happiness can be achieved through wealth, or power, or social position, or simply likeability and popularity. But Aristotle said, "No." These are all externals and can be taken away; they are too undependable. True human happiness comes from within.

In order to locate this interior principle, we must take note of a key word in Aristotle's thinking: *aretē*, usually translated *virtue*. Virtue is not, as we misunderstand the word today, moral uprightness or sexual continence. Rather, virtue to Aristotle is *excellence*, or more precisely *the power to become excellent*. Our word "virtuoso" is a closer approximation. A virtuoso on the violin is admired not only because he can play a difficult instrument well, but because he has disciplined the many motivations within him to *become* the excellent player he is. It is this power within the violinist, which he has brought under control, which sets him apart from the rest of us.

Of the human powers which we all share, the power of reason is the noblest. "Rationality is not merely the distinguishing feature of humanity; it is the best. 'If happiness is activity in accordance with virtue, it is reasonable that it should be in accordance with the highest virtue, and this will be the excellence of the best part of us.' "[15] Hence we arrive at the central Aristotelian principle of happiness: the exercise of reason in and for itself—the act of *becoming* rational—is the highest and noblest of all human endeavors. The "virtuoso in reason," in short, is the complete human being. Here is the "internal demon" whose fulfillment will lead to the sublimely happy life. Thus the man of thought and contemplation is the envy of all his fellows, for he has found the secret of happiness and well-being; he enjoys his own mind, revels in the beautiful satisfaction of human reason itself, and thus comes to know the humanly happy condition.

We are not about to reopen the question of whether or not Aristotle was right about all this. Rather, what presents itself to

15 Ibid., p. 63; quoted from Aristotle's *Ethics*, 1177ff.

us is the analogue which Aristotle's theory of human nature makes possible. This theory can be restated as follows: what makes man man is his reason. And since this is a power within, which he is free to exercise and develop on his own, it is the agency for achieving a genuine form of happiness on a self-governing basis. Happiness, then, does not come from *being* rational, but from *taking charge of one's own rationality,* cultivating and developing it, and *becoming* through it the rational animal one continually strives to be.

The analogue is simply this: what makes man man is the act of *taking charge of his own life.* And since this is not an abstract power belonging to some generic entity called "Man" but rather a personal and individual power belonging to you and to me as individuals, it is the "agency within" which, when exercised and developed, can lead to genuine personal identity and self-esteem. We are not saying happiness is the result, but something more like the sensation of being a *person,* self-moving, self-determining, unique, and therefore irreplaceable. We will leave to the philosophers and psychologists whether such a sensation is equivalent to happiness.

We are saying that the full human being for our time, beset by social conventions and bureautechnocratic requirements, is the individual who can be reminded that he possesses within himself the power of self-movement and self-definition, the power to become an *individual.* We believe that education must become the instrument for doing this reminding, and that once this renewed revelation is personally witnessed by each person, he can then become the free, self-identified person which his humanness specifies.

At this point, however, we need to know a little more about this "demon within" which we are trying to track down. In Chapter Four, we drew attention to Henry Aiken's view of man's peculiar position in the world. Man is uniquely the animal who knows he is going to die, and thus is capable of "making something beyond his own individual existence a matter of ultimate concern. This is something that escapes the rational animal as such." (And, incidentally, it explains why Aristotle was short of the mark in specifying the highest human quality as reason.) But more important, man is the self-perfecting, self-overcoming, self-transcending being. It is this quality about him which science can never know.

We speak of this quality as being somehow "within" the person. And it is not there in a social science sort of way, to be recorded and plotted on a graph and predicted and controlled. Rather, it is there in a phenomenal way; by that we mean that it is there in awareness. In each person, this center of selfhood, this point of origin for self-perfecting and self-transcending, is presented to our awareness as we move through the world. It is the business of a human education, as we shall see in Chapter Nine, to intensify this awareness and to bring it actively to the foreground of our consciousness.

Nietzsche had a word for it. He called it a mode of "self-surpassing," a quality of constantly doing oneself over, the "superman," the man superimposing upon his humanness his *own notion* of humanness! And this does not come from nature or the cosmos, but from his own self-generating powers of self-creation. "The truly educated (or rather self-educating) man— i.e., the superman or overman—is the man who is guided by the ultimate axiological goal of self-surpassing. . . . The self-surpassing man recognizes that this goal is only to be attained or, more precisely, asymptotically approached, through his own consistent effort and action."[16]

We in America have always found this Nietzschean notion about as inscrutable as Aristotle's idea of the "power of reason" somehow residing independently in a man's head, like a tiny god in a machine. We have distrusted pure reason because we have

[16] James W. Hillesheim, "Action and Solitude: A Nietzschean View," *Educational Theory* 19, no. 4 (Fall, 1969): 357.

found activism in the world more to our temperament. Our word is *intelligence* (not reason), by which we mean the application of reason to the world's affairs.

But this is precisely the point at which the Nietzschean self-surpassing man needs to get acquainted with his "demon within." For he cannot become an intelligent activist until he comes to terms with the mode of his own self-surpassing. And one of the ways he may do this, says Nietzsche, is through solitude and self-reflection. "The reason that Nietzsche recommends solitude to the man of affairs is not to deprecate action. Quite the contrary, to carry our 'superior actions,' to do great deeds—in short, to change the course of human events—this requires that one discover who he really is, what his capacities are, and then strive to *become* who he really is; it is only by acting in accord with one's potentials that one can achieve maximum effect in the world."[17]

HUMAN KNOWLEDGE

We see, then, that the "demon within" is the center of self-hood—more precisely, not the center but the point of origin for the knowing process. Knowledge begins to come into existence when a self sets out on the project of self-surpassing, of defining his own mode of "human-being-ness." And this means that knowledge, when all the shrubbery of science has been cleared away, is seen to spring from the *person*. The full impact of this assertion must now be analyzed, for it explains our position on epistemology as developed in this volume, and it supports our theory of education which is extrapolated in Chapter Nine.

Each man is unique. What a crashing cliché this has come to be! But what does it mean? Given our different heights and weights, varying colors of hair and eyes, assorted intelligence, temperaments, attitudes, outlooks, and aspirations, the repeat-

[17] Ibid., p. 359.

ability of any combination of these would certainly turn out to be awesomely unlikely. But no matter what the bookmaker's odds might read, this is not what we mean by uniqueness. We are unique not in a mathematical sense of escaping from the possibility of having a look-alike somewhere in the world. Rather, we are unique in the metaphysical sense: each one of us constitutes a once-and-for-all instance of a being engaged in the act of *becoming human*. And this act of becoming human is absolutely idiosyncratic in quality. It cannot be generic. It must be singular and individual.

Someone once said that each man must consider himself an exception to the rule. It was spoken as an injunction, but the breath was wasted. Each man already *does* consider himself such an exception. And this is what puts him ultimately beyond the reach of social science. For social science, like all science, understands things only through rules, as generalizations which characterize classes of objects. But each man is sui generis, literally in a class by himself; he is his own genus, and what can be said of him qua genus cannot then be uttered for any other. Social science is stopped dead in its tracks.

With the foregoing, it is now possible to specify the relationship between what we have called "the demon within" and the possiblity of "human knowledge." The relationship is this: man's uniqueness, his idiosyncratic mode of becoming human, is manifest principally through his power to know. Man's very knowledge of the world is a reflection of himself and his self-surpassing. Knowledge is man's stamp upon the world. What he likes to think of as truth is his own endowment of meaning upon his experience. Thus what man knows of the world is ultimately what he *wants* the world to be like.

This assertion is sufficiently heretical, in the community of modern-day epistemologists, to warrant an extended explanation. Man does not create the world, but he does create the world's meanings. There is the world, and there is knowledge of it. Man is responsible for bringing that knowledge into existence, into the world. If we concur with Immanuel Kant that the real world is forever beyond our reach, and if we accept Karl Popper's view that all we can ever be certain of is when we are wrong, then we may say that what we call "knowledge of the world" is, for all intents and purposes, what we mean by "the world." In this quasi-metaphoric sense we may say that man creates the world. And it is our contention that he creates it along dimensions of his own desire.

By way of illustration, consider John Dewey's five-step procedure comprising what he called "The Complete Act of Thought," perhaps his most widely celebrated contribution to epistemology, spelled out in *How We Think* (1910). In this analytic of the knowing process, Dewey claimed that hypotheses could be determined true or false, or, as he preferred, "warrantable" or "unwarrantable," by the consequences that would follow from acting on them. That is, to decide between Hypothesis A and Hypothesis B, the thing to do is to "consult experience" to see what happens when you go ahead with your life believing each of them to be the explanation to your problem. However, Dewey never went on to say how we should choose between the consequences themselves, between the experiential consequences of having acted on Hypothesis A and those of having acted on Hypothesis B. We are not told how to make *this* judgment as between the phenomena of the consequences themselves, it being assumed, apparently, that that decision would somehow take care of itself.

But this is precisely the zone in which human preferencing, human opting, human choosing is decisive. Here, at the juncture of deciding what kind of consequences we *like* and eventually what kind of world we *want*, all of our cognitive questions start on the long road to being answered and thus being turned into knowledge. The point is that we are required to first make a determination on what we want the world to be like before we decide whether a putative answer to a question is indeed an answer. We must have opted for a set of consequences preferred before declaring that a hypothesis reputed to be able to lead to those consequences is to be preferred over another which does not. In short, we must somehow "know," perhaps in a precognitive way, what kinds of conditions an answer must be able to satisfy before we can start producing answers to the questions we put to the world, i.e., producing knowledge. We may call this awareness precognitive because we cannot fully grasp its contents *until* we begin to make judgments of knowledge claims on the basis of it. But once we do, we awaken to the fact that our ideas become knowledge only when seen against the backdrop of a preferred set of conditions.

The question can be raised as to whether these preferences, these choices of wanted conditions which must be made before knowledge-seeking can proceed, shall count as a form of knowledge. Our considered answer would have to be a conditional "Yes." In one sense they represent the most human of all knowledge, for they originate phenomenologically in ourselves, in our awareness of ourselves in the world and what we want to make of that existential condition.

To illustrate, human beings have already endowed upon their world the norm of *Order*. We want the world to be the kind of place where a "rational approach," as we say, is likely to yield some results. We like to think of ourselves as rational beings, and this preference makes no sense unless we can also posit that the world in which we live is a rational place. Thus, before any search for knowledge gets under way, we have already set the ground rules for what shall count as knowledge: it must be of the sort which a rational being can find out in a rational universe.

Having made this primitive choice as to what kind of world we would like to be living in, we go on to subsidiary options. We believe, for example, that rational knowledge is, among other things, theoretical knowledge. That is, we can examine the stream of occurrences in our experience and slowly begin to collect them into larger and larger classes and groups, so that generalizations and laws can be formulated. This kind of thinking is what we have arbitrarily chosen to identify with the adjective *rational*. To be rational is generalizing upon our experience, rather than uttering an ad hoc truth about each event.

Finally, we convert this subsidiary option into a working principle: to be rational is to be scientific. Science is the mode of knowing which has a capability for generalizing upon and "making sense of" a stream of occurrences, bringing order to an unassimilated universe of phenomena.

We have thus closed the circle. We *want* the world to be an Order. Our reason, we believe, is capable of apprehending order and reason in the universe. Our reason is manifest in our science. Science, therefore, is the only kind of knowledge which lets us *know* the world we have chosen to believe is out there. In this way we see that *knowledge is the product of desire.*

To return to our question, is the preference for an Order in the universe—the preference itself—an instance of knowledge? We believe it is. But where did this knowledge come from? Our only hope for answering this question is to be prepared to accept the fact that it did not *come from* anywhere; it emerged phenomenologically in the human being. I want the world to be an Order. That desire on my part is a truth which I personally endow upon my world; it has no warrant, for it cannot be proven or disproven. But the fact that I do want the world to be that way is the primary condition which I legislate before I begin any act of knowing. I want the world to be the kind of place where scientific knowledge is true, and this desire is the first piece of knowledge I have to work with, even before I set out on scientific inquiry.

A second illustration of how man creates the world along dimensions of his own desire may be drawn from the work of Marjorie Grene. A long tradition in Western common sense has been, she writes, that in the fact-value duality we feel that fact comes first. That is, we believe that values somehow depend upon prior fact. One cannot judge an event, a situation, or a work until some facts about that thing have first been gathered. In-

deed, we *ought not* make such a priori judgments, for "getting
the facts" first is somehow an unarguable obligation in the Western tradition. It turns out, however, in Professor Grene's thinking,

> that our judgments of fact depend on constitutive judgments of
> value, not the other way around. Indeed, what was true in the
> assertion of the duality of facts and values was the insight:
> that values cannot be elicited from "bare" facts. The fact that
> a person called Beethoven on such dates wrote such marks on
> paper does not by itself account for the existence of the *Eroica*
> as a musical composition. . . . Only by an evaluation do we call
> the Eroica "music," not noise, and so assimilate the "fact" of its
> composition to the history of music rather than to acoustics.[18]

What goes for Beethoven, she says, must now be seen as applicable to all propositions. She argues that "all statements of fact,
however free of evaluation they may seem, are possible *only*
when some fundamental act of appraisal has already legislated
for the manner of their entertainment, formulation and assertion . . . even the least evaluative, most 'factual' judgments
depend for the possibility of their existence on some prior evaluative act."[19]

Or consider, she suggests, the working scientist. It is a cliché
by now, one that we all know too well, that the scientist is expected to remove his own personal biases, as much as possible,
from his investigation. He wants to be dispassionate, objective,
supremely disinterested, in a personal sense, in the outcome of
his experiments. But this, Professor Grene argues, is precisely
the point—the scientist is making a value assertion in his desire
to be all these things: "If all knowing is essentially a kind of
doing, and human doing is always value-bound, then knowledge is so as well. . . . The *objectivity* of human perception
which underlines all scientific accuracy and all canons of evi-

[18] Marjorie Grene, *The Knower and the Known* (New York: Basic Books,
1966), pp. 159–60.
[19] Ibid., p. 160.

dence, whether in scientific or historical disciplines, is an *objectification,* the result of a commitment to withdrawal."[20] Thus the scientist *chooses* to be personally separated from his investigations; he chooses to close off his personal hopes for the outcome, because he wants to live in a world where truth is not "infected" by personal desires. But this is his *desire!* This is the world he *wants* to dwell in, a world where smaller desires do not get in the way. "Again, what is involved here is the 'projection of the world,' not simply the habituation to a changed environment. And the development of scientific theories, each of which both relies on and modifies its predecessors, consists in the multiplication of mutually harmonious projections of this same essential kind. To become a competent specialist in any one branch of science is to participate with one's whole intellectual being in such a projection. . . . "[21] In simpler language, scientists create their world in their own image. They project upon the world the conditions they want to see there. These are the conditions they want because these are the conditions that make science possible. Since they want science, not only for their daily bread but as a matter of human concern, they demand the conditions. They thus project their own preferences upon the world; they bring a world into existence of their own choosing and desire.

Our argument, therefore, is that even science is a form of personal knowledge, personal in the sense that it springs from personal desire and choice. It so happens a great many people share in that desire, but a large company wanting something does not make that thing objectively wanted. On the contrary, it makes that thing subjectively, phenomenologically wanted.

That is our argument. Human knowledge is what we *want* to know. If the scientists can get away with imposing their own projection on the world, then it should be possible to entertain other projections originating from other quarters. Suppose, for

[20] Ibid., p. 179.
[21] Ibid., pp. 179–80.

example, that instead of removing ourselves so antiseptically from our investigations, we carry on our investigations by viewing ourselves as part of the problem. Suppose, to be even more precise, that a social scientist is studying the social and political effects of integrating a school system. Certainly he cannot treat his data as so many numbers on a chart or curves on a graph. They are that, of course, but their meaning is not given in their facticity. Their meaning is endowed upon them by the investigator's own phenomenological awareness of what is going on in the community; this awareness is always a product of his own personal situation, both as person and as social scientist.

Are the interpretations he arrives at and the conclusions he draws from his data knowledge? Of course they are. Knowledge does not come into existence by itself. It is brought into existence by a human being, even if he is working with data from essentially nonhuman phenomena. His data are data, and only that. His conclusions are knowledge, and a human knower must intervene in order to convert data into knowledge.

We speak, then, of human knowledge as the product of human beings engaged in the act of experiencing the world in and through their own personal preferences. All the social science presently housed in the university library (to take just one area of scholarship) has been written up and published by human investigators. To say that this vast body of knowledge is the product of the investigators' desire is not to discount or discredit it; all knowledge is that way. But we must read it in a new light. We should, if we had the funds, pull it all out of the library and republish it with a large footnote on the first page of every document elaborating the investigator's own personal history— where he came from, his attitudes, feelings, and prejudices, his thoughts on what man is, what Justice is, indeed, what research and scholarship themselves consist of. If we had time for such footnotes, we would then be in much better position to understand what he means by his article or book or essay.

But this is what we require in order to assimilate what he has found out as *human knowledge*. And this is the kind of knowledge, we hope, which may some day find its way increasingly into the school, where a human education may become the countervailing force which will humanize life in a bureautechnocratic society.

CHAPTER 9

Human Education

CONTEXT FOR A NEW EDUCATION

With the foregoing arguments in place, we are now in a position to sketch the outlines of a new educational theory. Theories, it should be said, are not put forward as portraits of reality. They are, instead, simply tools of analysis which purport to assist understanding. That is to say, theories are neither true nor false; they are simply useful or not so useful in comprehending some area of human activity. Perhaps the following will add another sliver of light.

In discussing the educational ideas of Michael Polanyi, James W. Wagener remarks that "the educated mind exhibits a moral dimension in the fact that it seeks guidance from its own creations."[1] If this is true, it stands as a "high definition" instance of the "two-edged sword" cliché. For man has created bureautechnocracy, with its trappings of clattering machinery, rational system, and depersonalized and feeling-free science; for the last fifty years, he has been "seeking guidance" from this monster of his own making. It is our thesis in the present volume that he has

---

[1] James W. Wagener, "Toward a Heuristic Theory of Instruction: Notes on the Thought of Michael Polanyi," *Educational Theory* 20, no. 1 (Winter, 1970): 53.

sought rather too well, and that in responding to the guidance offered by bureautechnocracy, he has permitted his moral dimension to be twisted out of shape.

But the sword's other edge is this: if man can seek guidance from one "creation," he can seek it from another. If bureautechnocracy can somehow be infused with a more generous ethic, we may look forward to more generous and humane guidance to issue from it.

The incipient beginnings of such an ethic may be detected in man's tentative probes into a form of knowing which runs beyond —somehow eludes the reach of—science. In Chapter Eight, we suggested the general character of this kind of knowing, and indicated that there is a certain precognitive quality to it. Its products are somehow "known" before actual thinking begins, and precisely because of its primitive, almost a priori character, this mode of knowing precedes and serves as gatekeeper for all subsequent (as the empiricists say) input. Or, to change the figure, this mode of knowing is the primary lens through which all subsequent experience must be gathered; it shapes and edits the knowledge that is taken in later through more systematic procedures—in school, for example. It is therefore critical in understanding the education of the person.

THE PHENOMENOLOGY OF
EDUCATIONAL EXPERIENCE

This primary, precognitive form of knowing has only recently been, one might say, "discovered."[2] It has lain beneath the awake and aware learner in school, not visible to the teacher and not detected even by the learner himself.

[2] As we write this, Charles Reich's *The Greening of America* (New York: Random House, 1970) has just appeared. The nameless kind of knowing to which we allude Reich labels *Consciousness*. Specifically, Consciousness II people come to know a world different from that of Consciousness III people.

Contemporary existential psychology has undertaken a study of it under the general rubric of "phenomenology." This term, made current by the German philosopher Edmund Husserl, refers to the kind of apprehending best captured by our ordinary term "awareness." The phenomenologist's argument can be put something like this:

> Philosophers can never be sure that either the world exists or that they, as human beings, exist. It would be very difficult, however, to fault the claim that in our "natural attitude" of encountering the world, something called consciousness occurs. But consciousness is always intentional; that is, it is always consciousness *of* something. Consider, then, these two terms: "consciousness" and "something." Consciousness without intentionally, that is, without the "somethings," is the province of psychology. On the other hand, the "somethings" without the presence of consciousness is the province of traditional metaphysics. What we are after is a reality lying somewhere between psychology and traditional metaphysics, somewhere between non-intentional consciousness and the world which we are conscious of. We shall call this region *phenomena*, an admittedly elusive term which is derived from a Greek word meaning "that which presents itself." Hence, the best we can do is to say that phenomena are the primitive features of the world which present themselves to our consciousness.[3]

This idea must be brought down from the lofty rhetoric of a learned journal into more understandable form. Perhaps an example will help. Michael Polanyi, for instance, speaks of "the tacit component." He refers to such a prosaic, but unappreciated, phenomenon as an individual being alert to certain features of his experience and disregarding others. Being attentive to X and unattentive to Y immediately predisposes the learner to a pejo-

[3] Van Cleve Morris, "Is There a Metaphysics of Education?" *Educatonal Theory* 17, no. 2 (April, 1967): 145.

rative assignment of higher rank to X over Y, and this is already on its way to becoming a form of "truth" in his makeup. And if one were to ask him why X takes precedence over Y, why it is more real in the foreground of his life, he would be unable to answer. Existentially it is just there, and he has put it there by a precognitive act of assignment. To cite another illustration, consider the commonplace remark, "he knows more than he can tell." There was a time, in the recent history of educational psychology, when such a claim would have been dismissed out of hand. If you cannot verbalize it, said the cognition experts, then you don't know it! But this dictum no longer holds. We are prepared to believe now, although earlier we were not, that the person, in the far reaches of his personhood, had hold of some kind of private comprehension which, while it searches for expression, can claim the status of knowledge. Some things a person *knows* cannot be *uttered*.

We have a dramatic, contemporary example of this: the so-called "black experience." Although blacks have known it for a long time, the remainder of society is now beginning to understand that the experience of being black in twentieth century America, in and of itself, is a unique psychological dynamic to which only some individuals are privy. This dynamic, this transaction between the person and his environment, leaves a deposit of awareness which can never be fully communicated to the white man. And this awareness, although not really expressible and therefore shareable—sometimes not even among blacks themselves—is absolutely primary in the structure of a black man's knowledge. It is the ground from which all his experience is gathered, and it therefore is absolutely necessary in understanding how a black man comes to know a world controlled by whites. At an unsophisticated level it is manifest in a black's conception of a policeman. He sees there, as few whites do, potential repression and brutality. This is his truth. At a more sophisticated level, it is revealed in the intellectual's demand for "black sociology" or "black psychology." The black experience tells you that social science, phenomenologically speaking, is either black or white and not the disinterested, objective, value-free "quest for truth" it has always been advertised to be.

Keep in mind that the above is only an illustration of a larger idea. There are other phenomenologies: of maleness, of femaleness, of youngness and oldness. There is indeed a phenomenology of bureautechnocracy which, we have claimed in this volume, has settled down over the school and the young people attending it, shaping their outlooks and devaluing their self-perceptions. It is this phenomenology which the educator is required to understand and modify. And how does he understand it? He must understand it by invading it, exploring it, participating in it, *feeling* it.

Why does an elementary youngster so readily submit to the teacher's notion of the curriculum and what should be learned at any given moment? It is because he has been brainwashed into believing that his own curiosities are subordinate to what the bureautechnocratic culture, by way of the teacher, has determined in advance that he should be curious about. He is overwhelmed by The System and has little confidence in his own judgment, and he is too young and helpless to protest.

Why does a secondary school student do his homework, take his tests, and grind away at his teachers' assignments, only to drop out in disgust before his diploma is reached? It is because his brainwashing is wearing off. He still is intimidated into believing that his own judgment is subordinate to that of the curriculum makers, but his powerlessness to change things leads him to the conclusion that his only form of protest is disengagement.

Why does a college student dutifully attend his classes in rhetoric, western civilization, and biology and then join a protest demonstration for greater relevance of his learning? It is because his brainwashing did not completely "take." He arrived at college thinking his studies were going to be different from high school, but they turned out to be the same kind of thing. However, he is older now. He is an adult among adults, and he is no longer intimidated by his lack of seniority in the system. For the first time, he is *in* and *of* the system, and he knows he has something to say about how it should work. So he protests.

This is the phenomenology of the person asserting itself against the phenomenology of bureautechnocracy; since it appears most dramatically in an educational setting, it is the education profession which is obligated to take first cognizance of it.

NEW ENDS FOR EDUCATION

What the young are saying, and what the educator himself is beginning to sense, is that the aims and ends of education are once again in need of overhaul. We all know that rethinking the aims of education is one of the most tired exercises in American educational literature. We used to argue—in the learned journals and the public prints—whether the schools' chief task was to train the mind or to develop useful skills of work and citizenship. There was enough in Greek educational philosophy to support both positions. Then we moved on to a kind of populist, Jacksonian synthesis and called it "life adjustment education." This had the ring of anti-intellectualism to it, so we reshaped it into a more intellective form and called it "education for the training of intelligence and problem-solving ability." Since intelligence is the application of thought to life, this kind of formulation satisfied both the Aristotelian rationalists and the Deweyan pragmatists.

But now we see that even this compromise is running out of gas. The student today simply does not want to be "intelligent." He resists it because to be intelligent in this sense is to be rational, coolly detached from the texture of life. He wants to be "cool," which in the strange inversions of popular argot now means to be involved and committed, two terms which unfortunately have already achieved the status of clichés.

Our own formulation might run something like this: students today want to be *engaged*, not like transmission gears but like lovers. They want involvement with life in the sense of being implicated personally in what is going on about them. This means that they want their learning to be relevant, not in the prosaic sense of being merely current but rather in the sense of making them aware of and responsive to other people's experience. In short, they want to *feel* their education, to be touched at a level of sensitivity which transcends the cognitive and fires the subjective.

One of the clearest manifestations of this can be found at the college level where the "outreach" effort, the struggle to make contact with the wider society, is now at its most active development. In their dealings with the so-called "community," colleges and universities are discovering that the people they hope will be their new clientele are not interested in what has traditionally passed for scholarship. Such scholarship represents the rational approach, aggressively disinterested and dispassionate. It is, almost by definition, irrelevant. It is double-domed, esoteric, other-wordly and so rejected. What is wanted are interested and passionate scholars who are oriented to participation, interaction, and concern. These terms, to the academic man, are empty; they are merely social categories. But to the new educational client, they represent education; they are the vehicle for learning. And, in this case, it is easy to see that the "teachers," i.e., the students and professors who go into the community to do their "interacting," will be the learners; the clients will be the teachers.

In any event, education must now turn from a precious tradition of detached scholarship and abstract truth to personal knowledge and human feeling. It is a demand not only of the students but of the times. There is, in a sense, enough "purefied" knowledge in the world, enough truth of the abstract, generalized, universalized sort. What we need is knowledge of a different kind, a knowledge not so pure, not so supremely true that it cannot inform a lived life now in progress somewhere in the world. We are not claiming, as the song says, that "what the world needs now is love, sweet love"; rather in a less sentimental way, that what the world needs now is personal knowledge and human response.

We arrive at a new focus for educational effort: personal significance. And we put the criterion forward without delay. *If an experience expands awareness and intensifies personal significance, it is educational.*

This new, somewhat unorthodox, educational aphorism obviously requires an extended gloss. We offer three representative qualities such an experience might be expected to provide: (1) a heightened feeling for other people's phenomenology; (2) an intensification of one's own sense of personal responsibility; (3) an expansion of affective curiosity.

Other people's phenomenology. One of the first requirements of the new education for personal significance will be to awaken in the individual a full-powered awareness of his own phenomenology. He must come to terms with his own fundamental predispositions as they have been formed within him, literally without his knowledge, in the process of growing up. He does this, however, by the indirect route of going outside, confronting other people's predispositions and through them confronting his own. To recall the "black experience" example discussed above, some whites lament that they do not want to be forced to think in terms of black and white, that they want to encounter people as people. But this is precisely the point—they do not realize they are incapable of doing so until their sensibilities have been shaken and they see that their phenomenal world has not included the feelings and sensations of being black.

To take another example, the social scientist studying ethnic minorities, say the urban Puerto Rican or Mexican-American, is typically unaware of the predispositions regarding these people which he brings with him to his work. Which means that before he can qualify as a legitimate student of a culture different from his own, he must involve himself personally in that culture in order to lay his assumptions, his feelings, out on the table and force himself to become aware of them in his own makeup.

To take a final, somewhat more troublesome example, the scientist of any subject matter is typically unmindful of his own predispositions and a priori assumptions, not as a person but *as a scientist*. Because he removes his own interests from the *conclusions* of his work, he has deceived himself into thinking that his own interests do not color his *assumptions*. But of course they do. If a scientist were to lay open his scientism, he would discover that his science produces knowledge because he has already given his endorsement to the process of inquiry which he uses, and that this endorsement is his own phenomenological act and is not necessarily shared by other individuals with other phenomenological backgrounds.

What all of this means is that the youngster in school or the adult in college must be required to make an assessment of his own feelings and attitudes, and then to compare those with the feelings and attitudes of others, in order to arrive at what the phenomenologist considers a very simple truth—that each man sees the so-called real world through his own prism. Until we get a good look at the prism in front of our own eyes, we cannot really see anything else very clearly.

Personal responsibility. It is a commonplace by now that a bureautechnocratic upbringing produces in us a kind of group-authority malaise. We are taught, throughout our maturing years, that morals are socially determined and that ethical response is legitimated not by the individual in his own private wisdom but by the corporate body, the culture, through its contemporary, transpersonal conventions. If a problem comes up, we are taught not to trust our own feelings and judgments in the matter but to turn instead to the mores and ethical rules of the wider society.

The effect of all this is not necessarily to make the wrong decision, but—whatever the decision—to assume that we have no *personal* stake in the problem's outcome. If things go wrong, we feel no obligation to blame ourselves; instead, we say that such and such was expected of me and that "I had no choice." It is this breakdown in personal answerability which is perhaps the first business of the new education to correct.

In today's schools, this a-responsible attitude has been urged upon us by, of all people, John Dewey and the latter-day Progressives. In the thralls of this outlook, we

> have fallen in love with the doctrine of sociality, and in our passion have allowed the school to become the arena where we demonstrate the great superiority of the group mind over the individual mind. All the darling children of the doctrine of sociality—group process, social promotion, the "whole-child" concept, the project method, psychodynamics—all these have been put into educational operation because of our great abiding belief that the *group* thinking, the *group* considering, the *group* choosing is a more authentic and reliable avenue to true humanity than the *individual* thinking, considering, and choosing.[4]

Thus the school has unwittingly become over the last couple of generations the place where children lose the sensation of personal choice. Instead, they are taught a kind of "Group Think" in the solemn name of classroom democracy. The effect of this is a subtle but very damaging surrender by each child of a part of his identity. For to choose the group's way, even if democratically arrived at, is an empty gesture, because the group's way by definition cannot be wrong. For the individual child to go the group's way is a form of passive experience. Even though he may have had a hand in deciding it, he cannot really see it as *his* way; it is always "out there," external to his own private life and adopted only on a kind of Rousseauian social contract basis.

Michael Polanyi once remarked that "you can neither believe

---

[4] Van Cleve Morris, "Freedom and Choice in the Educative Process," *Educational Theory* 8, no. 4 (October, 1958): 237.

nor disbelieve a passive experience. It follows that you can only believe something that might be false."[5] He meant by this that there is a personal thrust to all knowing, a reaching out as well as a taking in, a conscious appropriation with some risk involved. To know something is not merely to attend to it and nod your head, but to gather it in and call it *yours*. To know something is *to believe it to be true*. And you can only do this when it might be false.

The pedagogical lesson we must learn from this is that the youngster in today's bureautechnocratic schools is not given the opportunity to believe things "that might be false." Without that experience, he cannot really *personally* commit himself to anything he learns. Through the curriculum, but most especially through a new artistry of teaching, he must be brought back to a personal encounter with his own learning so that after each learning episode he understands clearly that what he believes to be true is not the school's truth, or the teacher's, but *his*.

The expansion of affective curiosity. The return to *belief* as a form of learning requires a parallel movement away from a preciously pure cognition toward gut-level passion. Teachers have known for a long time that the interest of the learner is absolutely essential to the success of learning. But they have always interpreted the word "interest" as an intellective, cognitive phenomenon; to be "interested" in something was to move toward it in order to comprehend it, to assimilate it mentally. Mortimer Adler used to speak of "the passion to know" as if it were a purely rational category.

What we must now rediscover is that the passion to know is a passion. "Knowing is one's way of being open to the world."[6] It is a desire to enter into a new and untried relationship with "reality," a search for new experiences with truth. And that

[5] Michael Polanyi, *Personal Knowledge* (New York: Harper Torchbooks, 1964), p. 313.
[6] Wagener, "Toward a Heuristic Theory of Instruction," p. 48.

means new kinds of belief. Our definition of "interest," therefore, must be restated as *the desire to have new experiences and through them to believe new things.*

This is what we mean by "affective curiosity"—the surge toward new feelings. It is not an alien concept by any means. It is illustrated every day in our schools. Why is it that, generally speaking, kindergarteners and first-graders love to go to school but secondary school students do not? The answer seems to us very simple. The very young are awakening to new *feelings* about the world; that is what "going to school" means to them. It is a sensation, literally, of having one's selfhood enlarged by introducing new feelings and responses into everyday life. And what about the high-schooler? He has lost this ecstacy because his teachers themselves have lost it. They do not consider feelings a legitimate concern of instruction; so far as they are concerned, education is all cognition and mastery. The youngsters catch this change in attitude and gradually detach themselves from any interest in learning.

The kind of passion we are talking about occasionally reappears at the upper end of the educational track, at the graduate, Ph.D. level. Here, sometimes, the students are awakened by the same affection for learning, for plunging into a problem for the sheer joy of understanding it better. Whether he knows it or not, the scholar has feelings, not just as a person but as a scholar. He is a scholar because he "gets a charge" out of knowing, he tingles when he understands. Every new comprehension changes his relationship with his world, and he enjoys the new feelings which those changes ignite.

A NEW PEDAGOGY

With these notes on the ends of education completed, we turn now to the conversion of these ends into a working model of instruction. And, although much teaching and learning occurs beyond the school's walls, we are taking the liberty of confining our specifications to the public school. This institution is still the most powerful vehicle for bringing the young to that circumstance of "personal significance" which we have described and annotated above. Furthermore, it is in the public school that we have gone wrong, and it is in the public school that the majority of educational reforms are needed. We shall order this discussion around three general topics: (1) the curriculum as the "personification of knowledge"; (2) the teacher as the New Socrates; (3) the learner as the Significant Person.

The Curriculum as the "personification of knowledge." We borrow this phrase from George Kneller of U.C.L.A.[7] Our reading of it goes something like this. The teacher necessarily functions as a mediator between the curriculum and the learner. This mediation is not merely of the "conveyor belt" sort; rather, it is better understood through the metaphor of the "personal messenger." The teacher stands to the learner as a bearer of a kind of "news," represented by the curriculum. But, in this case, teaching is not merely journalism. Journalism is the bearing of news with no affective regard for the impact of that news on one's listeners or readers. The reporter's loyalties lie with the news itself, rather than with the subjectivities to whom he speaks or writes. Walter Cronkite is emphatic about it: "We must never, never, never consider the consequences that our information will have on people or on ourselves."[8] The teacher, on the other hand, bears news with his eyes on the receivers; it is their reactions to the information which take first place in his attention. In just this way, good teaching differs from good journalism.

To look at the curriculum as "news" is to draw attention to a new dimension of the learning process, the meaning and signifi-

---

[7] Developed in a paper entitled "Education, Knowledge, and the Problem of Existence," delivered before the Philosophy of Education Society in 1961.

[8] "What Does Walter Cronkite Really Think?" *Look*, November 17, 1970, p. 60.

cance of that "news" in the life of the one who learns it. By way of example, Neil Sutherland of the University of British Columbia offers the study of history.

> The study of history in the school . . . should follow a procedure identical to that used by the professional historians. . . . History is an inductive study and historical method an inductive method. The historian collects his data and subjects it to processes which he calls external and internal criticism. These steps in his method, however, draw attention to a very peculiar characteristic of the historian's data: it is the historian himself who decides what his data are. From the mass of existing documents and remains he selects only those which he believes to be historically significant; he decides which of them are historical "facts" and which are not. . . . In making his choices, in his analysis, and in his subsequent narration of his conclusions, the historian is obliged to bring to bear every bit of knowledge, skill and intelligence which he can muster. . . . Nevertheless, since any historical situation is made up of an infinite number of variables, the historian is able to isolate and analyze only a small fraction of them; sooner or later he must decide what he believes happened and why he believes it happened, and set his conclusions down for his colleagues to criticize. School history studied in this way would provide countless "exercises" in choice.[9]

Sutherland goes on to say that if the pupil were to study the history of, say, his hometown or his nation in this way, he would discover "for himself those underlying assumptions of his society which he must understand before he can declare himself free of them." The pupil would also be liberated from the so-called "Third Person," i.e., the personality of the author of the textbook who steps in at the last moment and saves the reader from the necessity of self-decision and self-responsibility.

[9] Neil Sutherland, "History, Existentialism, and Education," *Educational Theory* 17, no. 2 (April, 1967): 173–74.

In a very literal sense, therefore, Mark Antony and George Washington and Adolf Hitler are not just biographies to learn about, but problems to be figured out. The pupil, as historian, would approach an understanding of these men and their achievements by reconstructing their histories and concluding for himself just where they stood in the pantheon of mortals who have, as they say, "made history." The point is that the pupil, having achieved this understanding on his own, would then appropriate this historical subject matter as *his*. His conclusions might be false, but as we have seen that is what makes it possible for the pupil to believe them as true. It is a case of converting object matter into genuine *subject* matter, matter which a subjectivity can commit himself to as knowledge.

The teacher as the New Socrates.   The role of the teacher is implicit in the foregoing commentary on the curriculum. His task is to encounter the person of the learner and to assist the person to examine subject matter from his own perspectives. Perhaps the oldest example of this kind of teaching is that of Socrates. However, the Socratic paradigm is ambiguous because Socrates himself showed a certain deviousness in his method. In many of the question-asking episodes for which he became famous, he knew in advance what the correct answer was, and he was dogged in his determination to extract it from his student. Thus, after tedious but persistent interrogation, he was able to squeeze the Pythagorean theorem out of the slave boy, one of the mini-heroes of *The Meno*. But it is quite obvious that the slave boy had no personal interest in that theorem, nor did he make any move to incorporate it into his life. In this sense, therefore, Socrates' teaching was technically successful, but humanistically a failure.

It is in another mode of Socratic dialogue that we find the key for a teacher of the new education—namely, in those episodes wherein Socrates did *not* know the answers to the questions he was raising. With his pupil Plato he believed that there *was* an answer somewhere in the realm of Ideal Forms, but we can dismiss this metaphysics as not necessarily limiting in the present discussion. For the fact of the matter is that he taught *as if* he did not know the answers, and it is this kind of teaching which brought his students personally into the act of learning. When he asked them, "What is justice?" they had to wrestle with this problem themselves as genuine inquirers, and not just as answer-boys. When they were done, not knowing what justice really was, they at least knew that they did not know, which to Socrates was the first step toward self-understanding.

One of the continuing sadnesses of American education is that it has provided so little room for these kinds of questions. The youngster—at almost any level of the educational ladder—has virtually no opportunity to express his own idiosyncratic response to the things the school teaches him. His responses are not important, except as they correspond with the established questions to which the system has already worked out the answers. Charles Silberman, in his recent study of American schools,[10] speaks of them as "joyless." They are joyless not because there is an absence of recreation or educational games; they are joyless because a child cannot experience the joy of personal discovery, and we mean by that not only the discovery of some objective truth but also the discovery of his own feelings about that truth as it seeks to enter his life.

The new education will require a massive dosage of Socratic dialogue. This prescription is not made lightly. It is the one chance we have of rescuing our schools from a bureautechnocratic joylessness by which they have been captured.

The Learner as the Significant Self.   We do not intend ending this volume with some sentimental essay on the beauty and exquisiteness of the individual person. Education in America has already had plenty of that kind of rhetoric. Instead we offer a portrait of the learner in our schools which is free of sweet

[10] Charles Silberman, *Crisis in the Classroom* (New York: Random House, 1970).

treacle and effete preciousness. It is the picture of the learner that we might want painted of ourselves as persons. We want self-determination; so does the learner. We want self-esteem and significant identity; so does the learner. We want to stand against the bureautechnocratic environment, to assert our own lives as alternatives to its requirements; so does the learner.

But the learner, of course, is only learning how to *be* these things. He needs the kind of teaching which will assist him in seeing how one *comes to be* this kind of person. We have offered some clues above as to the strategies a school and its teachers might follow to provide this kind of instruction. But strategies are for institutions, not for individuals. Persons do not use strategies on each other; it is a contradiction in terms. Persons *are* something to each other. They open themselves as individuals to others. In the case of the learner, he is anxious to open himself to his teacher, because that self is in formation. As such, it is supremely and compellingly interesting to him, and he wants not only to share it but to enlarge it with the encounter with the teacher.

This idea has been persuasively developed in an unpublished paper, "Existential Teaching," by Austin Patty of Oregon State University. Professor Patty argues that the basis of authenticity is really nothing more complicated than candor and honesty with one's own selfhood. The teacher cannot really teach authenticity; all he can do is *be* authentic. And in being authentic, he exhibits a mode of personal existing which the pupil may see on view every day. The pupil is therefore in a position to catch this mode, to feel it, to respond to it, and eventually to *be* it himself. Patty speaks of the dynamic between teacher and student as *the exchange of introspections*. The teacher and the pupil simply open themselves to each other—their feelings, their doubts, their fears, their joys, their sadnesses, their laughter. In this trade, they come to know not the mind of the other but the person of the other. The mind's contents can be appreciated later, the teacher's obviously greater than the learner's. But maybe this differential is not so important, and perhaps the pouring of the knowledge from the one into the vessel of the other is not so urgent as we have customarily insisted. It can wait.

The emergence of the significant person comes from other quarters. We suspect that it comes largely from the learner taking charge of his own learning; in effect, becoming the architect of his own curriculum. As in the case of history cited above, the schoolman may have a better idea than the learner of all the knowledge that presently exists in the world; but the learner is absolutely autonomous when it comes to deciding what that knowledge means, and how it fits into a life being lived in this place in this hour by this person. He is the only agent in the educative process who is in a position to convert knowledge into meaning.

And that, after all, is what education is all about. For it is only through the development of personal meaning that the sense of individual significance can be built up. And we do not offer this in a simply psychiatric sense. We are saying that the sense of identity, the feeling of self-esteem, the sensation of being a significant person is achieved not merely through sensitivity sessions and group therapy, although in special instances they may be helpful, but rather through a day-by-day assumption of power by the learner over the course of his own learning. We see this most vividly today in our colleges and universities where the cry for relevance really means the cry for self-direction. It is manifest in the so-called Alternate University being thrust forward on the nation's campuses by the Hartford Committee; in their literature the Committee affirms, among other things, that "education which has no consequences for social action or personal growth is empty."

It is this "personal growth" theme to which education must now turn. The world has enough scientists, enough technicians, enough secretaries, enough organizers, managers, and coordinators. What it needs now are persons. A bureautechnocratic culture stands against men in the development of personhood. A human education can help the learner to stand against that culture, to assert his own idiosyncratic qualities of direction and style, and to establish his own private meaning in a public world.

There is nothing essentially mysterious about the sense of personal significance. It lies within us all the time, except that today it is in a weakened condition. We have been talked out of it by an anti-man culture. We can work our way back to it through a human education.

BIBLIOGRAPHY

Addams, Jane. "The Public School and the Immigrant Child," *Proceedings of the National Education Association,* 1908, pp. 99–102.

Aiken, Henry David. "Morality and Ideology," in Richard T. George, ed., *Ethics and Society: Original Essays on Contemporary Moral Problems.* Garden City, N.Y.: Doubleday Anchor Books, 1966.

———. "'Rationalism, Education, and the Good Society," *Studies in Philosophy and Education* 6 no. 3 (Summer, 1968): 249–281.

Allport, Gordon W. *Becoming: Basic Considerations for a Psychology of Personality.* New Haven: Yale University Press, 1955.

Bennis, W. G.; Benne, K. D.; and Chin, R., eds. *The Planning of Change.* New York: Holt, Rinehart and Winston, 1968.

Bennis, W. G., and Slater, P. E. *The Temporary Society.* New York: Harper and Row, 1968.

Brameld, Theodore. *Philosophies of Education in Cultural Perspective.* New York: Holt, Rinehart and Winston, 1955.

Bredemeier, H. C., and Toby, Jackson, eds. *Social Problems in America.* New York: John Wiley and Sons, 1960.

Brennan, Joseph G. *The Meaning of Philosophy.* New York: Harper and Row, 1953.

Bronowski, Jacob. *The Identity of Man.* Garden City, N.Y.: Natural History Press, 1966.

Broudy, H. S.; Smith, B. O.; and Burnett, J. R. *Democracy and Excellence in American Secondary Education.* Chicago: Rand McNally, 1964.

Brumbaugh, Robert S., and Lawrence, Nathaniel M. *Philosophers on Education.* Boston: Houghton Mifflin, 1963.

Cleaver, Eldridge. *Soul on Ice.* New York: McGraw-Hill, 1968.

Cubberly, Ellwood. *Public School Administration.* Boston: Houghton Mifflin, 1916.

DeCarlo, Charles R. "Perspectives on Technology," in Eli Ginsberg, ed., *Technology and Social Change.* New York: Columbia University Press, 1964.

De Gre, Gerard. *Science as a Social Institution.* New York: Random House, 1955.

Dewey, John. *Democracy and Education.* New York: Macmillan, 1916.

———. *Experience and Nature.* New York: Dover Publications, 1958.

———. "Individuality, Mediocrity, and Conformity in Education," in Carl H. Gross et al., *School and Society.* Boston: D. C. Heath, 1962.

———. *The Quest for Certainty.* New York: Menton, Balch, 1929.

Ellul, Jacques. *The Technological Society.* Trans. John Wilkinson. New York: Alfred A. Knopf, 1964.

Erikson, Erik H. *Childhood and Society.* 2nd ed. New York: W. W. Norton, 1963.

———. *Identity: Youth and Crises.* New York: W. W. Norton, 1968.

Frankel, Charles. *The Case for Modern Man.* Boston: Beacon Press, 1959.

———. *The Democratic Prospect.* New York: Harper and Row, 1962.

Freud, Sigmund. *Civilization and Its Discontents.* London: Hogarth, 1953.

Friedenberg, Edgar. *Coming of Age in America: Growth and Acquiescence.* New York: Random House, 1963.

———. "Current Patterns of Generational Conflict," *Journal of Social Issues* 25, no. 2 (Spring, 1969): 21–38.

———. *The Dignity of Youth and Other Atavisms.* Boston: Beacon Press, 1965.

———. *The Vanishing Adolescent.* Boston: Beacon Press, 1964.

Fromm, Erich. *Escape from Freedom.* New York: Rinehart, 1941.

———. *The Sane Society.* New York: Holt, Rinehart and Winston, 1955.

Galbraith, John Kenneth. *The New Industrial State*. New York: New American Library, 1967.

Ginzberg, Eli, ed. *Technology and Social Change*. New York: Columbia University Press, 1964.

Girvetz, Harry K. *The Evolution of Liberalism*. New York: Macmillan, 1963.

Goodman, Paul. *Growing up Absurd*. New York: Random House, 1956.

Grene, Marjorie. *The Knower and the Known*. New York: Basic Books, 1966.

Gustafson, Donald F., ed. *Essays in Philosophical Psychology*. Garden City, N.Y.: Doubleday, 1964.

Hacker, Andrew. *The End of the American Era*. New York: Atheneum, 1970.

Handlin, Oscar. *The Uprooted*. Boston: Little, Brown, 1951.

Harrington, Michael. *The Other America: Poverty in the United States*. Baltimore: Penguin Books, 1962.

Henry, Jules. *Culture against Man*. New York: Random House, 1963.

Hickerson, Nathaniel. *Education for Alienation*. Englewood Cliffs, N.J.: Prentice-Hall, 1966.

Hodgkinson, Harold L. *Education in Social and Cultural Perspectives*. Englewood Cliffs, N.J.: Prentice-Hall, 1962.

———. *Education, Interaction, and Social Change*. Englewood Cliffs, N.J.: Prentice-Hall, 1967.

Hook, Sidney. *John Dewey: His Philosophy of Education and Its Critics*. New York: Tamiment Institute, 1959.

———. *Political Power and Personal Freedom*. New York: Macmillan, 1959.

Horney, Karen. *The Neurotic Personality of Our Time*. New York: W. W. Norton, 1937.

Huntington, S. P. "Conservatism as an Ideology," *American Political Science Review* 51 (June, 1957).

Hutchins, Robert M. *Education for Freedom*. Baton Rouge: Louisiana State University Press, 1943.

Huxley, Aldous. *Brave New World*. New York: Harper and Brothers, 1958.

Itzkoff, Seymour. *Cultural Pluralism and American Education*. Scranton, Pa.: International Textbook Company, 1969.

Jacobson, Lenore, and Rosenthal, Robert. *Pygmalion in the Classroom.* New York: Holt, Rinehart and Winston, 1968.

Jourard, Sidney M. *The Transparent Self.* Princeton, N.J.: Van Nostrand Company, 1964.

Kaplan, Abraham. *The Conduct of Inquiry: Methodology for Behavioral Science.* San Francisco: Chandler, 1964.

Keniston, Kenneth. *The Uncommited: Alienated Youth in American Society.* New York: Harcourt, Brace and World, 1965.

Kimball, Solon T., and McClellan, J. E. *Education and the New America.* New York: Random House, 1962.

Knowles, Louis L., and Prewitt, K. *Institutional Racism in America.* Englewood Cliffs, N.J.: Prentice-Hall, 1969.

Lichtheim, George. *The Concept of Ideology and Other Essays.* New York: Random House, 1967.

Litt, Edgar. *Beyond Pluralism: Ethnic Politics in America.* Glenview, Ill.: Scott, Foresman, 1970.

Lundberg, George A. "The Postulates of Science and Their Implications for Sociology," in Maurice Nathanson, ed., *Philosophy of the Social Sciences: A Reader.* New York: Random House, 1963.

MacIver, R. M. *Social Causation.* New York: Harper and Row, 1964.

Mack, Raymond W. *Transforming America: Patterns of Social Change.* New York: Random House, 1967.

Marcuse, Herbert. *An Essay on Liberation.* Boston: Beacon Press, 1969.

———. *Eros and Civilization.* Boston: Beacon Press, 1954.

———. *One–Dimensional Man: Studies in the Ideology of Advanced Industrial Society.* Boston: Beacon Press, 1964.

Maslow, Abraham. *Religions, Values, and Peak Experiences.* New York: Viking Press, 1970.

———. *The Psychology of Science.* New York: Harper and Row, 1966.

Mason, E. S. *The Corporation in Modern Society.* Cambridge: Harvard University Press, 1959.

Matson, Floyd W. *The Broken Image: Man, Science, and Society.* Garden City, N.Y.: Doubleday Anchor Books, 1966.

McLuhan, Marshall. *Understanding Media: The Extensions of Man.* New York: McGraw-Hill, 1964.

Minogue, Kenneth. *The Liberal Mind.* New York: Random House, 1963.

Mitgang, Herbert, ed. *The Letters of Carl Sandburg.* New York: Harcourt, Brace, and World, 1968.

Molnar, Thomas. *The Decline of the Intellectual.* New York: World Publishing Co., 1961.

Myrdal, Gunnar. *Challenge to Affluence.* New York: Random House Vintage Book Edition, 1965.

Nathanson, Maurice, ed. *Philosophy of the Social Sciences: A Reader.* New York: Random House, 1963.

National Association of Manufactures. *Calling All Jobs.* New York, October, 1957.

Packard, Vance. *The Status Seekers.* New York: Pocket Books, 1959.

Pappenheim, Fritz. *The Alienation of Modern Man.* New York: Monthly Review Press, 1959.

Phenix, Philip H. *Realms of Meaning.* New York: McGraw-Hill, 1964.

Polanyi, Michael. *Personal Knowledge.* New York: Harper Torchbooks, 1964.

Rogers, Carl. *On Becoming a Person.* Boston: Houghton Mifflin, 1961.

————. "Toward a Science of the Person, in T. W. Wann, ed., *Behaviorism and Phenomenology.* Chicago: University of Chicago Press, 1964.

Rogers, Carl, and Coulson, W. R., eds. *Man and the Science of Man.* Columbus, Ohio: Charles E. Merrill, 1968.

Roosevelt, Theodore. "Keep up the Fight for Americanism," *El Grito: A Journal of Contemporary Mexican-American Thought* 1, no. 2.

Rosen, Bernard; Crockett, H. J.; and Nunn, C. Z., eds. *Achievement in American Society.* Cambridge, Mass.: Schenkman, 1969.

Roszak, Theodore. *The Making of a Counter Culture.* Garden City, N.Y.: Doubleday, 1969.

Ryle, Gilbert. *The Concept of Mind.* New York: Barnes and Noble, 1949.

Scheffler, Israel. *Science and Subjectivity.* New York: Bobbs-Merrill, 1967.

Schellenberg, James A. "The Class-Hour Economy," in Dorothy Wesby-Gibson, ed., *Social Foundations of Education.* Glencoe, Ill.: The Free Press, 1967.

Sexton, Patricia. *The American School: A Sociological Analysis.* Englewood Cliffs, N.J.: Prentice-Hall, 1967.

Sherif, M. *Group Relations at the Crossroads.* New York: Harper and Row, 1953.

Silberman, Charles E. *Crisis in the Classroom.* New York: Random House, 1970.

Skinner, B. F. "Freedom and the Control of Man," *American Scholar* (Winter, 1955–56).

————. *Science and Human Behavior.* New York: Macmillan, 1953.

————. *The Technology of Teaching.* New York: Appleton-Century-Crofts, 1968.

Slater, Philip. *The Pursuit of Loneliness: American Culture at the Breaking Point.* Boston: Beacon Press, 1970.

Smith, F. V. *Explanation of Human Behavior.* 2nd ed. London: Constable, 1960.

Stein, M. R.; Vidich, A.; and White, D. M., eds. *Identity and Anxiety: Survival of the Person in Mass Society.* Glencoe, Ill.: The Free Press, 1960.

Steinberg, Ira S. *Educational Myths and Realities: Philosophical Essays on Education, Politics, and the Science of Behavior.* Reading, Mass.: Addison-Wesley, 1968.

Swados, Harvey. "The Myth of the Happy Worker," in Maurice Stein et al., eds., *Identity and Anxiety.* Glencoe, Ill.: The Free Press, 1960.

Titus, Harold. *Living Issues in Philosophy.* 4th ed. New York: American Book Company, 1964.

Tyack, David B., ed. *Turning Points in American Educational History.* Waltham, Mass.: Blaisdell, 1967.

Watson, Goodwin. "Resistance to Change," in W. G. Bennis, K. D. Benne, and R. Chin, eds., *The Planning of Change.* 2nd ed. New York: Holt, Rinehart and Winston, 1968.

Wheelis, Allen. *The Quest for Identity.* New York: W. W. Norton, 1958.

Winetrout, Kenneth. *F. C. S. Schiller and the Dimensions of Pragmatism.* Columbus: Ohio State University Press, 1967.

Young, Michael. *The Rise of the Meritocracy, 1870–2033: Essays on Education and Equality.* Baltimore: Penguin Books, 1961.

INDEX

Addams, Jane: quoted, 142–43
Adler, Mortimer, 211
Administration, deans of, 168
The Adolescent Society, 143
Advertising: functions of, 42–44; and science, 183–84
Aiken, Henry, 190; quoted, 96, 101–2, 104, 111–12, 113
Alcoholics Anonymous, 133
Alienation, 3, 65n
Allport, Gordon: quoted, 106–7
Alternate University, 218
American Association of Colleges for Teacher Education, 168
American Council of Learned Societies, 168
American ethos: and bureautechnocracy, 13
American Humanist Association, 167n
American Management Association, 62
Americans: obedience of, 186
Anger, 128
Anomie, 40–41
Antony, Mark, 215
Anxiety, 3
Aristotle, 188–89, 191
Asch, Solomon, 185
Associated Organizations for Teacher Education, 168
Attitudes: and bureautechnocracy, 24
Automobile safety, 28

Barret, William: quoted, 153
Becoming: quoted, 106–7
Beehive, analogy of, 51–57
Beethoven, Ludwig van, 197
Behavior: controlling, 91–94; and sci-

entific methodology, 121; and ideas, 129–30; control of and science, 134–36
Behaviorism: quoted, 91
"Black experience," 204–5, 208. *See also* Negroes
Brameld, Theodore: quoted, 150–51
Brave New World: quoted, 91–92
Bredemeier, H. C.: quoted, 78
Brennan, Joseph G., 129
Buddhism, 131
Bureaucracy: and schools, xi–xii; defined, 4; and U.S. Army, 4–5; and education, 154–58
Bureautechnocracy: benefits of, ix; and values, x–xi, 24; and freedom, x–xi; defined, 3, 7, 161–62; as an environment, 7–11; and American ethos, 13; origins of, 13–16; consequences of, 16–24; and social man, 21; and the individual, 23–24; and attitudes, 24; and repression, 45; and choice, 50–51; and long-range goals, 57–58; and labor, 61–63; and loss of self-esteem, 67–83; and man as instrument, 68–73; and expendability of man, 73–77; and alienating conditions of work, 74–77; and material goods, 77–80; and scientific liberalism, 103–15; and science, 121–22, 131–36; and schools, 137–58, 163–64, 205–6

California, University of, 67
Capitalism, 13
The Case for Modern Man: quoted, 98–99